READINGS ON

BLACK BOY

OTHER TITLES IN THE GREENHAVEN PRESS LITERARY COMPANION SERIES:

AMERICAN AUTHORS

Maya Angelou
Stephen Crane
Edith Wharton
Emily Dickinson
William Faulkner
F. Scott Fitzgerald
Robert Frost
Nathaniel Hawthorne
Ernest Hemingway
Herman Melville
Arthur Miller
Eugene O'Neill
Edgar Allan Poe
John Steinbeck
Mark Twain
Walt Whitman
Thornton Wilder

AMERICAN LITERATURE

The Adventures of
  Huckleberry Finn
The Adventures of Tom
  Sawyer
The Call of the Wild
The Catcher in the Rye
The Crucible
Death of a Salesman
Ethan Frome
Fahrenheit 451
A Farewell to Arms
The Glass Menagerie
The Grapes of Wrath
The Great Gatsby
Heart of Darkness
Of Mice and Men
The Old Man and the Sea
One Flew Over the Cuckoo's
  Nest
Our Town
The Pearl
The Scarlet Letter
A Separate Peace
To Kill a Mockingbird

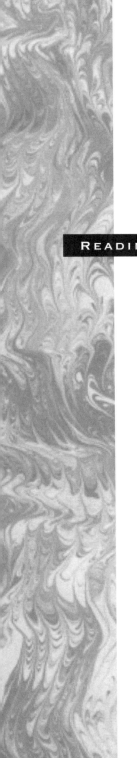

THE GREENHAVEN PRESS
Literary Companion
TO AMERICAN LITERATURE

READINGS ON

BLACK BOY

Hayley Mitchell, *Book Editor*

David L. Bender, *Publisher*
Bruno Leone, *Executive Editor*
Bonnie Szumski, *Series Editor*

Greenhaven Press, Inc., San Diego, CA

Every effort has been made to trace the owners of copyrighted material. The articles in this volume may have been edited for content, length, and/or reading level. The titles have been changed to enhance the editorial purpose. Those interested in locating the original source will find the complete citation on the first page of each article.

Library of Congress Cataloging-in-Publication Data

Readings on Black boy / Hayley Mitchell, book editor.
        p.   cm. — (The Greenhaven Press literary
    companion to American literature)
        Includes bibliographical references (p.   ) and index.
        ISBN 0-7377-0243-5 (lib. : alk. paper). —
    ISBN 0-7377-0242-7 (pbk. : alk. paper). —
    1. Wright, Richard, 1908–1960. Black boy. 2. Authors,
    American—20th century—Biography—History and
    criticism. 3. Afro-American authors—Biography—
    History and criticism. 4. Afro-American youth—
    Biography—History and criticism. 5. Wright, Richard,
    1908–1960—Childhood and youth. 6. Autobiography—
    Afro-American authors. I. Mitchell, Hayley, 1968–   .
    II. Series.
    PS3545.R815Z813   2000
    813'.52—dc21   99-16774
    [B]   CIP

Cover photo: Archive Photos
Library of Congress, 31

Copyright © 2000 by Greenhaven Press, Inc.
PO Box 289009
San Diego, CA 92198-9009
Printed in the U.S.A.

66 *Again and again I vowed that someday I would end this hunger of mine, this apartness, this eternal difference; and I did not suspect that I would never get intimately into [other's] lives, that I was doomed to live with them but not of them, that I had my own strange and separate road, a road which in later years would make them wonder how I had come to tread it.* *99*

Richard Wright,
Black Boy

CONTENTS

Chapter 1: Structure and Style in *Black Boy*

1. Richard Wright's *Black Boy:* A Twentieth-Century Slave Narrative *by Sidonie Ann Smith*   34

Black Boy is similar to early African American slave narratives, whose subjects refused to accept their oppression as fate or the masking of true feelings that enabled such acquiescence. Like these slaves, Wright is willing to rebel against discrimination and oppression to the point of annihilation in order to retain a true sense of self.

2. Narrative Structure of *Black Boy* *by John O. Hodges*   43

Wright's autobiography follows the traditional structure of a bildungsroman, a German term for a work that recounts a young man's education or formation of character. Wright's work is special, however, in that his character is formed within a society that is repressive, restrictive, and antagonistic.

3. Richard Wright Sings the Blues *by Ralph Ellison*   55

While the work of Richard Wright shows the influence of some of the world's great literary figures, *Black Boy*, in some of its technical qualities and tone, is also influenced by the tradition of Negro blues.

4. *Black Boy* Is Incomplete Without *American Hunger* *by Janice Thaddeus*   58

This essay seeks to clarify the odd publishing history of *Black Boy*, a book which, in this author's opinion, should not have been changed from its original form.

5. *Black Boy* as Art *by Charles T. Davis*   69

Wright's autobiography details his dreams of becoming an artist; the work represents his fulfillment of that dream. The reconstruction of his painful childhood is a supreme artistic accomplishment despite the fact that his critics often favor other works.

Chapter 3: The Black Experience

FOREWORD

The story's bare facts are simple: The captain, an old and scarred seafarer, walks with a peg leg made of whale ivory. He relentlessly drives his crew to hunt the world's oceans for the great white whale that crippled him. After a long search, the ship encounters the whale and a fierce battle ensues. Finally the captain drives his harpoon into the whale, but the harpoon line catches the captain about the neck and drags him to his death.

A simple story, a straightforward plot—yet, since the 1851 publication of Herman Melville's *Moby-Dick*, readers and critics have found many meanings in the struggle between Captain Ahab and the whale. To some, the novel is a cautionary tale that depicts how Ahab's obsession with revenge leads to his insanity and death. Others believe that the whale represents the unknowable secrets of the universe and that Ahab is a tragic hero who dares to challenge fate by attempting to discover this knowledge. Perhaps Melville intended Ahab as a criticism of Americans' tendency to become involved in well-intentioned but irrational causes. Or did Melville model Ahab after himself, letting his fictional character express his anger at what he perceived as a cruel and distant god?

Although literary critics disagree over the meaning of *Moby-Dick*, readers do not need to choose one particular interpretation in order to gain an understanding of Melville's novel. Instead, by examining various analyses, they can gain numerous insights into the issues that lie under the surface of the basic plot. Studying the writings of literary critics can also aid readers in making their own assessments of *Moby-Dick* and other literary works and in developing analytical thinking skills.

The Greenhaven Literary Companion Series was created with these goals in mind. Designed for young adults, this unique anthology series provides an engaging and comprehensive introduction to literary analysis and criticism. The essays included in the Literary Companion Series are chosen for their accessibility to a young adult audience and are expertly edited in consideration of both the reading and comprehension levels of this audience. In addition, each essay is introduced by a concise summation that presents the contributing writer's main themes and insights. Every anthology in the Literary Companion Series contains a varied selection of critical essays that cover a wide time span and express diverse views. Wherever possible, primary sources are represented through excerpts from authors' notebooks, letters, and journals and through contemporary criticism.

Each title in the Literary Companion Series pays careful consideration to the historical context of the particular author or literary work. In-depth biographies and detailed chronologies reveal important aspects of authors' lives and emphasize the historical events and social milieu that influenced their writings. To facilitate further research, every anthology includes primary and secondary source bibliographies of articles and/or books selected for their suitability for young adults. These engaging features make the Greenhaven Literary Companion series ideal for introducing students to literary analysis in the classroom or as a library resource for young adults researching the world's great authors and literature.

Exceptional in its focus on young adults, the Greenhaven Literary Companion Series strives to present literary criticism in a compelling and accessible format. Every title in the series is intended to spark readers' interest in leading American and world authors, to help them broaden their understanding of literature, and to encourage them to formulate their own analyses of the literary works that they read. It is the editors' hope that young adult readers will find these anthologies to be true companions in their study of literature.

INTRODUCTION: IS *BLACK BOY* REALLY AUTOBIOGRAPHY?

Richard Wright's *Black Boy* has been acclaimed as both the finest autobiography by an African American and one of the greatest American autobiographies ever. Readers of *Black Boy,* however, often have trouble distinguishing its genre, as it does not seem to follow the rules of autobiography, telling the whole truth and nothing but the truth. Yet it likewise is clearly not straight fiction.

With the blurring of fact and fiction in the work, one often does not know what to accept as truth and what to accept as melodrama and fantasy included for the sake of a good story. Some critics of Wright's day, such as African American W.E.B. Du Bois, were concerned about the authenticity of the work. "The subtitle, 'A Record of Childhood and Youth,' makes one at first think that the story is autobiographical," Du Bois says. "It is at least in part. But mainly it is probably intended to be fiction or fictionalized biography. At any rate the reader must regard it as creative writing rather than simply a record of life."[1]

Though readers can never be sure to what extent Wright did blend truth and fantasy, Margaret Walker, a friend of Wright and one of his biographers, claims that most of the incidents he recounts in his autobiography are verifiable. Though he "embroidered and embellished and even exaggerated" she says, "they are truth as Wright chooses to render truth."[2] It is this use of both autobiography and fiction, Walker says, that makes the book less a literary form than a piece of ingenious art.

The fictional techniques that Wright employs throughout the book include but are not limited to dialogue, scene, irony, and the use of heightened emotional tone to create suspense for the reader. Wright also renders himself as a character in the book; although he writes the book in the first person ("I"), he does so with a kind of objective detachment usually reserved for fiction. As an autobiography, the work is unique in this light. "The most important distinction *Black Boy* bears," contemporary Wright scholar Yoshinobu Hakutani writes, "is Wright's intention to use the young self as a mask. The attitudes and sentiments expressed by the young Wright are not totally his own but represent the response of those he called 'the voiceless Negro boys' of the South."[3] Finally, Wright does not simply write a chronological account of his youth in *Black Boy*, giving happy and unhappy incidents equal weight and drama. He *chooses* which incidents best illustrate his messages about poverty, racism, and survival.

However one defines its form, the subject of *Black Boy*, the subject of the bulk of Wright's work, is clear. And that chief subject, biographer Keneth Kinnamon explains, is "the racial problem, and his chief importance is as an interpreter of it in imaginative literature." Furthermore, Kinnamon adds:

> No black writer between Frederick Douglass and James Baldwin has offered so moving a testimony or uttered so scathing an indictment of the American racial situation to so large an audience as has Richard Wright. To have done so in spite of such enormous odds as Wright faced during his childhood and youth is not only a literary and social achievement, but also a profound witness to the capacity and the endurance of an exceptional human spirit.[4]

The essays in this volume both illuminate the human spirit of Richard Wright and convey an understanding of the writing techniques, themes, and sociological issues of *Black Boy*. Some contemporary critics continue to explore Wright's craft, from his use of narrative structure to the influence of the blues in his work. Other critics focus on issues of identity, strength, and rebellion, discussing, among other things, the role of racism in both Wright's journey to adulthood and his literary apprenticeship. Readers will find that these topics and many others in this collection offer a varied and exciting introduction to criticism on Richard Wright and *Black Boy*.

NOTES

1. Quoted in Yoshinobu Hakutani, "*Black Boy:* A Record of Childhood and Youth," in *Richard Wright and Racial Discourse.* Columbia: University of Missouri Press, 1996, p. 114.
2. Margaret Walker, *Richard Wright: Demonic Genius.* New York: Warner, 1988, p. 190.
3. Hakutani, "*Black Boy,*" p. 116.
4. Keneth Kinnamon, *The Emergence of Richard Wright.* Urbana: University of Illinois Press, 1972, p. 162.

RICHARD WRIGHT: A BIOGRAPHY

Growing up in poverty in the racist South at the start of the twentieth century, Richard Wright was an unlikely candidate for literary fame. A onetime Communist and eventual expatriate, his life was one of both intense struggle and great professional acclaim. He became, against immense odds, America's first best-selling black author. Critically acclaimed for his writing, his work has influenced generations of African American writers and readers of all races.

STRUGGLE AT AN EARLY AGE

Richard Wright was born on September 4, 1908, in Roxie, Mississippi, to Nathan Wright, a sharecropper, and his wife, Ella, a schoolteacher. Although both his parents were working, when Ella delivered her second child, Leon Alan, in September 1910, the family found that they could not afford to keep their farm running as well as take care of the boys. To lessen the financial burden, (a year later) Richard's mother moved with her sons to Natchez to live with her mother. Nathan, in the meantime, remained separated from the family, working odd jobs, until he secured a position with a sawmill.

In light of his history of struggle, it seems fitting that the first memory of this early period recounted in Wright's autobiography, *Black Boy*, is not a happy memory, but one that symbolizes much of his later strife. While living in his grandmother's house, Richard, who was nearly four years old at the time, set fire to her kitchen curtains, then hid underneath the house to avoid punishment. His convalescing grandmother needed to be evacuated, and his mother panicked when Richard could not be found. When he was discovered, she beat him severely.

Wright biographer Michel Fabre explains that this experience was the first of many in childhood that wounded Richard, as he regarded his severe punishment as a form of betrayal. "It not only seriously inhibited his independent spirit," Fabre writes, "but also caused him to doubt his relationship to his mother. How could the source and object of all love turn into a fury, capable of punishing him so painfully and rejecting him so totally? This episode brutally shattered the emotional security he had derived from the exclusive affection of his mother."[1]

ABANDONED BY FATHER, LIVING IN SHAME

While Richard questioned his relationship with his mother, he also grew apart from his father, who had been a sporadic presence in his life. When the family did regroup and moved to Memphis, Tennessee, in 1913, instead of becoming closer to his father, Richard resented him for working at night and sleeping during the day, an arrangement that forced Richard and his brother to remain quiet during daylight hours. Then, in 1914, when Richard was six, Nathan sealed his son's negative opinion of him forever. He abandoned his family for another woman.

Nathan's departure and his subsequent refusal to pay Richard's mother enough child support for them to live on was a source of shame for the family. Ella was shamed by being forced to take Nathan to court and also by asking her sons to beg him for money when the court's judgment was against her. Richard, in turn, was ashamed to have to face his father and his mistress, but he had enough pride at age six to refuse his father's money after having begged for it. Richard and his brother also had a sense of being outsiders. They were different from other children, their mother said, because now they did not have a father.

Although Richard's mother worked as a cook in a private home to support the family during this time, she was unable to make ends meet. The family went hungry for the first time in their lives. Wright biographer Addison Gayle notes that this hunger exacted both a physical and mental toll on Richard:

> To young Richard Wright, hunger brought home the full impact and consequences of the absence of the father he had grown to hate. For the first time in his life, the pain of hunger became constant, overpowering. It was unexplainable, frustrating, nerve-wracking. Whole days passed with scarcely more than bread and tea. The ability to play freely left him. He grew tense, nervous, morose.[2]

Not yet in school, Richard spent much of his time wandering the streets, thinking about food and his new responsibilities as the man of the house and caretaker of his brother. It was also during this period that Richard learned to fight to stick up for himself on the streets of Memphis and when, as he notes in *Black Boy*, he became somewhat of a drunkard after acquiring a taste for alcohol given to him for the be-musement of patrons at the local taverns he would frequent, looking for food and company.

A BRIEF OPPORTUNITY, THEN CHANGE AGAIN

Richard felt additional shame in his poverty when he attended school at Howe Institute in Memphis, for the first time at age eight. He remained a shy boy and he was fearful of speaking in front of others. Despite feeling inferior to the other children, Richard did make a few friends, from whom he learned various obscenities that would later get him into trouble at home as well as in the neighborhood. Just as he was starting to settle into a somewhat normal pattern at school, however, another crisis hit home. As would be the case with all his attempts at formal education, Richard's attendance at Howe Institute was interrupted. On this occasion, it was the sudden illness of his mother in 1916.

Richard dropped out of school to care for his sick mother, unaware that this was the first of a number of illnesses that would debilitate her for most of the rest of her life. Ella's illness crippled the already poverty-stricken family to the point of destitution. She lived off charity for a short while, then was forced to put Richard and his brother in a local orphanage for more than a month because she could not care for them.

Richard's brief stay at the orphanage served as another source of frustration and fear. The other children were bitter and vindictive, and he felt mistreated by the orphanage director, Miss Simon, after he refused to allow her to adopt him. When he tried to run away from the site, he was returned by a white police officer and beaten by Simon. Wright was not totally abandoned by his mother at this time. She did visit the boys frequently, beseeching them to have patience with her as she worked to improve her health and save enough money to allow them to leave Memphis.

Once Ella had saved enough money for the trip, she moved with the boys first to spend the summer with her parents, now living in Jackson, Mississippi, and then to Elaine, Arkansas, to live with Richard's Aunt Maggie and Uncle Silas Hoskins. Richard and his brother enjoyed the change of scenery during their summer in Jackson, but they lived under the rule of their devoutly religious grandmother, against whose strict authority Richard would soon rebel. When the family moved to Elaine, Richard felt more at home in his Aunt Maggie's house and enjoyed the attention of his Uncle Hoskins. This brief happy period was cut short by a racial killing that deeply affected Richard and changed the direction of his life yet again.

A LESSON IN RACISM FORCES ANOTHER MOVE

Silas Hoskins owned a saloon frequented by black sawmill workers in Elaine. In 1917, shortly after Richard moved in with his aunt and uncle, Silas was fatally shot in his saloon after ignoring the threats of white men who wanted to take over his property. Upon hearing that threats had been made on the entire family, Maggie and Richard's family fled to West Helena immediately. Before this incident, Richard felt wary toward whites; on the streets he had heard rumors of black men being beaten or killed by whites, but this was the first time he was aware of racism affecting him directly. What resulted was a new fear and hatred of whites: "This was as close as white terror had ever come to me and my mind reeled," Wright writes in his autobiography. "Why had we not fought back, I asked my mother, and the fear that was in her made her slap me into silence."[3]

Moving often between 1917 and 1919, the Wrights first settled again with Ella's mother in Jackson, then set off on their own to West Helena, where Ella soon suffered a stroke. Now paralyzed and unable to care for her sons, Ella returned to her mother in Jackson, Leon joined Aunt Maggie in Michigan, and Richard moved in with his Uncle Clark and Aunt Jody in Greenwood, Mississippi, near Jackson.

Although Richard was well provided for in Greenwood, he felt ill at ease in his uncle's home. He became overly sensitive about any criticism directed at improving him, and he carried feelings of guilt over his mother's suffering. Richard began to sleepwalk and seemed nearly on the verge of a nervous breakdown after learning that a young boy had previously died in the room he was occupying. Afraid of being in the house and becoming more and more difficult for his aunt and uncle to handle, Richard was sent again to live with his mother and grandmother in Jackson, where he would spend the remainder of his adolescence.

ADOLESCENCE IN JACKSON

Between 1920 and 1923, Richard attended three schools, worked a variety of odd jobs, and further developed an interest in reading that had been piqued previously by magazine adventure stories. The first of the three schools was a Seventh-Day Adventist school in Huntsville, Mississippi. His grandmother believed the Adventist school would be the best for Richard in that it would supplement the religious instruction he received at home, but he clashed violently there with his Aunt Addie, the devoutly religious teacher of his class.

Richard felt that the other children in Addie's class were dull and that the work was not challenging enough. Addie, on the other hand, felt threatened by Richard's boredom in class. She beat him in front of the other children to make an example of him, but Richard knew that the beating was without just cause. Later, when Addie tried to beat him at home, he defended himself with a knife, learning, Michel Fabre writes, "to overcome the authority of the family, discovering that violence would also earn him respect in the adult world."[4]

Rather than return to the Adventist school for the subsequent term, Richard was allowed to attend Jim Hill School, a public school in Jackson. He entered the school as a fifth grader but was soon advanced to sixth grade despite his relative lack of previous schooling compared with other children. Richard took joy in his success at the school and made friends among his classmates. In addition to these social successes, however, during his years at Jim Hill, Richard's poverty was apparent to everyone. His entire family was now living in poverty after having spent the last of their savings on medical specialists for Ella, who showed no signs of recovering from her paralysis. Richard's clothes were in tatters, he could not immediately afford his books and other supplies for school, and he often went hungry.

To earn a little money for food and necessities, Richard delivered newspapers and worked with a traveling insurance salesman, two jobs he recalls with some shame in his autobiography. Richard enjoyed selling the newspapers for the magazine stories that they included. He would sneak these works into his grandmother's house, where he had been forbidden to read anything other than religious material. He soon quit his newspaper route in shame, however, upon learning from the father of one of his friends that the paper was run by supporters of the Ku Klux Klan.

Richard's job as insurance salesman assistant likewise filled him with shame when he discovered that black families in the Mississippi Delta were being taken advantage of. In the Delta the plantation system flourished. The illiterate blacks of the region worked in the cotton fields and were forbidden education. Richard was depressed by the squalor of entire families living in one-room shacks. Addison Gayle notes that it was here that Richard "found unmistakable evidence of the human spirit crushed, of the desire for freedom not dormant but non-existent—and he hated it," referring to the people there as a "bare bleak pool of black life."[5]

In the fall of 1922 Richard returned to school, entering seventh grade at the Smith-Robertson Public School. He continued to earn money for books, food, and clothes by doing odd jobs such as running errands for whites. Over the year his interest in pulp fiction and magazine stories deepened, and he read every story that he could get his hands on. Among Richard's favorites were detective stories in Flynn's *Detective Weekly*, Agatha Christie's mysteries, Zane Grey's *Riders of the Purple Sage*, Jack London's adventure stories, and Edgar Allan Poe's detective works. These and other tales that remained forbidden in his household planted the seeds for Richard's first creative efforts which would soon be made public.

BITTERSWEET SUCCESS

During his eighth-grade year, when Richard was fifteen, he wrote his first short story, "The Voodoo of Hell's Half-Acre," which was serialized in three installments in the black newspaper *Jackson Southern Register* in 1924. As Wright describes it in *Black Boy*, the purely atmospheric story was about a villain who was after an elderly widow's home. The character of the villain was based on a neighborhood bully, James Biggy Thomas. It was a small first accomplishment, but one that Richard was proud of just the same, and something he erroneously thought might earn him respect among his family and peers.

Although Malcolm Rogers, the editor of the newspaper, liked Richard's writing and encouraged him to submit more work, neither Richard's family nor his community were impressed by his literary pursuits. Grandmother Wilson railed against Richard's use of "hell" in his title and believed that his soul was stricken for writing lies; as Wright notes in his autobiography, her opinion of all fiction was that it was "the devil's work."

Richard's mother likewise condemned his work, worrying aloud whether the story might prevent him acquiring a good job in the neighborhood. In addition, Richard's friends did not understand why he would want to write in the first place;

his work clearly had no value to those around him. Despite the lack of encouragement he received from others and his disappointment over not being paid for his work, Wright was pleased to see his work in print. Kinnamon writes that "the pleasures of authorship as well as the delights of reading had become for Wright a tactic for survival."[6]

Outside of his brief literary accomplishment, Richard continued to do well in his studies and in 1925 he graduated valedictorian of his ninth-grade class at Smith-Robertson. A minor disagreement occurred at the time between Richard and the assistant principal, W.H. Lanier, who had prepared a speech for him that would be sure not to offend important white school officials in attendance at the graduation. Richard refused to read the prepared speech, however, and delivered one of his own. He graduated, Kinnamon says, "tense, defiant, estranged from his black world and fearful of the white world he was about to encounter, but taking a grim satisfaction in his own integrity."[7]

After graduating with his ninth-grade class at age sixteen, Richard resolved to forgo further public education and to leave the deep South for Memphis, Tennessee. Instinctively, he seemed to know that life in Jackson could offer him little more than what he already had. "A black boy was boxed in by four alternatives in the deep South," biographer Margaret Walker writes:

> If he was not in school and had no job, he had to be either in the army or in jail. These were his options. Vagrancy or the semblance of what is put on the face of it was not tolerated in a black male. No standing on the corner, day or night was allowed, and black youths congregating in gangs on street corners were in open defiance of the law whether they knew this or not.[8]

With one hundred dollars in his pocket—most of which he had acquired through dishonest dealings at a local movie house—and a single suitcase in hand, Richard said good-bye to his mother, assuring her that he was leaving on his own accord, not because he was in some kind of trouble with Jackson whites. It was a proud moment for him, and although he was heading into unknown territory, he felt a new sense of freedom as he left his adolescence and Jackson behind.

WORKING IN THE WHITE WORLD

Soon after arriving in Memphis, Richard was able to benefit from previous experience working in an optical shop to get on at the Merry Optical Company as an assistant and delivery boy. He lived frugally during this time, eating poorly to save enough money to send for his mother and brother to join him. In addition to struggling to get by on his meager wage, Richard found that moving north had not alleviated all of his inner turmoil about whites. Though the whites in the Memphis were not violent toward blacks, racial tensions in his workplace were palpable. "Race hatred permeated the atmosphere," Gayle writes, "but it was buried under pretensions of urban smugness, covert, rendered more often through symbolic actions rather than overt ones."[9]

Blacks in the community did not face the strict Jim Crow laws of the deep South, but segregation was still practiced and Richard's freedom was still limited. His local library, for example, was closed to blacks. To indulge his passion for reading, Richard was forced to borrow books from whites until a white coworker lent him the use of his library card. Even then, Richard was forced to forge a note to the librarian, requesting that he be allowed to deliver the books to his employer.

For this episode, much recounted in Wright biographies, and also explained in some detail in *Black Boy*, Richard is known to have written: "Dear Madam: Will you please let this nigger boy have some books by H.L. Mencken."[10] The derogatory language that Richard chose for this note proves that he was deeply aware of the racist attitude of whites in Memphis, and that his position as a "nigger boy" was broadly accepted in the community at large.

DESIRING AND ACCOMPLISHING GREATER THINGS

The more literature Richard read in Memphis, the greater his desire to achieve literary success of his own. In addition to Mencken, writers such as Sinclair Lewis, Mark Twain, Joseph Conrad, Theodore Dreiser, and others inspired him to work toward leaving the South completely and finding a place where his aspirations to greatness could be realized. This opportunity arose between 1927 and 1928, when after saving enough money for his mother and brother to join him in Memphis, he set out for Chicago with his Aunt Maggie, to again find work and save to bring his family farther north.

In Chicago, Richard worked at a number of odd jobs before landing a part-time position with the postal service. After years of poor nutrition, however, he could not pass the physical exam (at age twenty, he weighed less than the required 125 pounds) to work there full-time. Regardless, he was making more money than he ever had in the past and was able to both save and eat regularly, and he soon had enough money for his mother and brother to move up from Memphis.

By the spring of 1929, Richard had gained enough weight to pass the postal physical, and he began work as a substitute clerk and mail sorter. His financial security was short-lived, as the impending stock market crash and the subsequent depression would put him out of work again in less than a year, but this period was an important one for Richard.

His family was secure in a larger apartment, and he was free to read and write more regularly. Richard also sought out the company of those who would better appreciate his literary yearnings than his family and immediate community by briefly attending meetings of black literary groups. He did not feel as though he fit in well with these groups, however, as he sensed their desire to achieve success as writers was less than his own. He accomplished more by writing in solitude at home.

In addition to producing a number of short stories at this time, he also began working on his first novel, called *Cesspool*, which ironically would become *Lawd Today*, his last novel, published posthumously. Of his work of this time Wright says, "My writing was more an attempt at understanding than self-expression. A need that I did not comprehend made me use words to create religious types, criminal types, the warped, the lost, the baffled; my pages were full of tension, frantic poverty, and death."[11]

THE DEPRESSION AND COMMUNISM

In the spring of 1930, Wright lost his postal job in a wave of layoffs following the stock market crash. He worked for a short time selling burial insurance to blacks, but, dismayed by the dishonesty of the profession, he quit to return to whatever odd jobs he could find. Eventually ending up on state relief funds, Wright later worked as a porter for the Michael Reese Hospital, mopping floors and cleaning the cages of experimental animals, and then for the South Side Boys' Club and Federal Negro Theatre.

Although his work life was unfulfilling and his family could now ill afford their large apartment, Wright did gain another small success in his literary life. His second publication, the short story "Superstition," appeared in *Abbott's Monthly Magazine*, a black journal. Wright wrote the story specifically for the magazine's audience, and he was later ashamed that it contained no worthy social or political commentary. What distressed him more at the time, however, was that, strapped by the depression, the magazine did not pay him the thirty dollars promised him for the story.

During these depression years, many of Wright's writer friends had gained an interest in Communist literary groups and had encouraged him to join. He remained skeptical at first, however, having seen the activities of the League of Struggle for Negro Rights, a radical Communist group in the African American community. Of this group Wright commented in *American Hunger*, part two of his autobiography:

> I liked their courage, but I doubted their wisdom. The speakers claimed that Negroes were angry, that they were about to rise and join their white fellow workers to make a revolution. I was in and out of many Negro homes each day and I knew that the Negroes were lost, ignorant, sick in mind and body. I saw that a vast distance separated the agitators from the masses, a distance so vast that the agitators did not know how to appeal to the people they sought to lead.[12]

Despite these feelings, Wright did eventually join his friends in attending another Communist group, the John Reed Club, in 1932.

In 1932 Wright was working as an insurance salesman and a street cleaner. He was forced to move his family into a dirty tenement. Depressed by these conditions, his affiliation with the literary John Reed Club in 1933 allowed him to escape the atmosphere of work and home. Here, he felt a sense of community that he had rarely felt elsewhere in his life.

THE JOHN REED CLUB INFLUENCE

Controlled by the Communist Party, the John Reed Club sought black membership during the depression, and its members welcomed Wright courteously and treated both him and his writing with respect. He was not required to join the Party on the basis of his club attendance, but the preamble of the club insisted, Kinnamon notes, that "the interests of all writers and artists should be identified with the interests of the working class."[13]

In addition to the companionship Wright gained through his club attendance, he also found a new outlet for his writings. The group was affiliated with the Communist Party magazine *New Masses* as well as *Left Front*, a journal devoted to writers at the early stages of their career. Wright soon began to regularly publish his poems and short stories in these and other leftist journals.

As Wright's publication credits in these journals grew between 1933 and 1934, his involvement in communism grew as well. Fabre explains that although Wright "was somewhat torn between his new sympathies and his mother's religious beliefs, he came to see in Marxism an organized search for truth about the life of oppressed peoples, and this convinced him that the Communists were sincere." [14] Thus, Wright joined the Communist Party after he was elected executive secretary of the Chicago John Reed Club in 1934; he also served as a member of the literary board of *Left Front.*

Much to his disappointment, Wright's involvement with the John Reed Club was cut short by the Party's decision to disband the club in the summer of 1934 in an effort to focus less on literary pursuits and more on political ones. Wright remained active in these other more political arenas of the Party. In addition, he was one of sixty-four writers to help found the American Writers' Congress in 1935. The first conference for the congress took place in New York in the spring of 1935, and while the event was run by the Communist Party, non-Communist writers were in attendance as well. Wright attended and gave a speech on "The Isolation of the Negro Writer," in which he stated:

> Some of the more obvious results [of isolation] are lack of contact with other writers, a lack of personal culture, a tendency toward escape mechanisms of ingenious, insidious kinds. Other results of his isolation are the monotony of subject matter and becoming the victim of a sort of traditional Negro character. [15]

Although Wright was becoming more well known for his writing, he still faced racism daily. Even while attending the conference, he was refused a room in a "whites only" hotel in Harlem. Despite this racial setback, his work there did lead to other things, as he was soon hired by the Federal Writers' Project to research the history of Illinois and of the Negro in Chicago.

RICHARD BEGINS TO MAKE A NAME FOR HIMSELF

In addition to working for the Federal Writers' Project, Wright helped organize the Communist Party–sponsored National Negro Congress, held in Chicago in February 1936. He was specially selected by the Party to preside over sessions on black history and culture. These literary activities gave Wright a chance to meet other notable African American writers, such as Langston Hughes, and encouraged him to write extensively.

In November, his own writing efforts paid off when his short story "Big Boy Leaves Home" appeared in the *New Car-*

avan anthology, where it attracted critical attention. It was the first time his serious efforts at fiction had been noticed outside of the Communist Party by the white press. Although the story did receive praise in Socialist papers such as the *Daily Worker* and *New Masses*, it was also lauded in the *New York Times* and the *Saturday Review of Literature.*

With the success of "Big Boy Leaves Home," Wright began to turn away from his poetry, which had appeared regularly in numerous journals, to focus on short-story writing. And while much of the fiction he sent out for publication was still rejected, in 1937 Wright decided to turn down a permanent position with the postal service to move to New York City to pursue his writing career.

In Chicago, Wright had begun to feel stifled by the Communist Party. He even withdrew his national Party membership at one point, while remaining connected to his local chapter. Now in New York, however, he found the Party to be more liberal and enlightened, so he reinstated his Party membership.

Soon after re-establishing his Party ties, Wright became the Harlem Bureau editor of the Party newspaper, the *Daily Worker.* Additionally, he helped launch the magazine *New Challenge,* which was in fact the continuation of a previously established journal titled *Challenge.* Wright also lent his writing talents to *New Masses* and the New York City Writers' Project, and he worked on what was soon to become his first published book of stories.

That book, published in 1938, was *Uncle Tom's Children: Four Novellas.* The theme of each of the novellas was racial conflict and violence, a theme that Wright would continue to explore in later works. The critical reception was sometimes harsh, but acclaim was widespread, including favorable reviews in both the scholarly and popular press and praise from black and white critics alike. Wright's story "Big Boy Leaves Home," which was a part of the collection, also won a $500 first prize from *Story* magazine, a journal that remains prestigious for both aspiring and well-established writers today. Other stories in the collection won individual awards as well, and within a year, Wright was awarded a Guggenheim fellowship, which gave him financial stability and allowed him the necessary time to complete his first published novel, *Native Son.*

A Brief Marriage

As the publication of *Uncle Tom's Children* and various awards marked his emergence into American literary celebrity, Wright was moving toward marriage in his personal life. He just needed to decide which of two women he would choose to marry: Dhimah Rose Meadman, a white classical dancer and divorcée with a two-year-old son, or Ellen Poplar, a white member of the Communist Party. He chose Dhimah, marrying her in August 1939, with African American writer Ralph Ellison serving as best man.

Soon after, the couple moved to Mexico with Dhimah's mother and son. Life in Mexico was said to be cheaper than in New York, and the new family hoped to escape the tensions of the early months of World War II (America had not yet joined the war). The arrangement seemed ideal for Wright, as he could write and live cheaply. What Wright found in Mexico, however, was that he was quickly swept up into an active social life, entertaining American visitors in his ten-room villa. Marriage to Dhimah did not meet Wright's expectations, either. Fabre explains:

> He had hoped to have more time with his wife, only to find that she reveled in this worldly and artistic circle of which she was the center. He suddenly discovered that Dhimah was preoccupied with herself, whereas he would have liked her to be more completely devoted to him. He now saw her as just as indolent and insensitive to him as she was to their servants and the natives.[16]

Thus, having found Dhimah's material lifestyle too bourgeois, Richard returned to the States alone in the summer of 1940, after just three months in Mexico. He divorced her before the end of the year.

NATIVE SON

If *Uncle Tom's Children* stirred up good press for Wright, *Native Son*, a novel of social protest, created a tidal wave of acclaim. When the book was published in March 1940, it became the first book by an African American writer selected for the Book of the Month Club. The national attention the novel received as a result boosted sales to over a quarter million copies in three weeks, making Wright the first best-selling black author in America. He was soon in demand for radio and magazine interviews, as well as lecture engagements nationwide.

Wright's concerns about the black community's reaction, despite some dissenting critics, were assuaged when James Ivy, speaking for the National Association for the Advancement of Colored People (NAACP) found nothing to criticize in his work. Wright also awaited the Communist Party response. As an affront to Wright, some Communist reviewers delayed their comments for a month. Some then claimed *Native Son* gave readers misleading impressions of the Party, and failed as a good source of Communist propaganda, which the Party felt Wright was duty-bound to produce in all his writings, but he was clearly rewarded elsewhere for his sense of craft.

In addition to its selection by the esteemed Book of the Month Club, the novel received critical praise from both the literary and popular press. Indeed, one reviewer likened Wright to John Steinbeck and Theodore Dreiser, writers he had admired during the early stages of his self-made literary education. Had Wright not gone on to write future novels, with *Native Son* he made an indelible mark in the history of American literature.

MORE LITERARY SUCCESS, WEDDING BELLS, AND BREAKING PARTY TIES

The year 1941 was a busy one for Wright. Amid the commercial and critical success of *Native Son* the previous year, Orson Welles had purchased the rights to turn the novel into a Broadway production, with Wright and writer Paul Green writing the script. In addition to working like mad to make last-minute revisions to the play at the beginning of the year, Wright also completed, with writer Edwin Rosskam, *Twelve Million Black Voices: A Folk History of the Negro in the United States*, which was published the same year.

Native Son, the play, opened on Broadway in March and ran through June for 115 performances in all. Though the play and its cast received mostly good reviews in the press, it did not attract enough theatergoers to break even. Despite the fact that the play lost money, the good press continued to enhance Wright's literary reputation. "The important papers praised the play on artistic grounds," Fabre writes, "the Left hailed it on ideological grounds and because it represented an innovation for Broadway, and even the Communist press was mostly favorable."[17] Hollywood came calling, too, when the Metro-Goldwyn-Mayer studio offered to buy the film rights. Wright rejected the offer, however, as the studio hoped to produce the film with white actors in the leading roles.

In addition to his continuing literary success, Wright's personal life improved in 1941 as well when he reunited with Communist Party member Ellen Poplar. The two married in March and moved into an apartment in New York. In April of the next year, their first daughter, Julia, was born.

Over the next three years, Wright continued to write for a variety of publications, and sections of his autobiography were accepted for publication by magazines such as the *Atlantic Monthly*. In these years he also gradually became less active in Communist activities, and in 1944, he broke from the Communist Party completely and published a two-part article about his experience in the Party in the *Atlantic Monthly* titled, "I Tried to Be a Communist."

In the article, Wright condemned individual Party members for the ill treatment he felt he had received from them in his later years with the group. "The article questioned the sincerity of the Communists," Fabre writes, "and revealed the 'terrorist' methods used at the very heart of the Party toward the somewhat undisciplined members, emphasizing the total scorn for individual liberty which such disciplinary action betrayed." [18] Wright's article drew immediate criticism from Party members. Some who had once been friends now rejected him outright; others chose not to denounce him but would not defend him, either.

BLACK BOY

As it turned out, Wright needed little defending, as the publication of his autobiography, *Black Boy*, guaranteed public favor. In speaking about *Black Boy*, Wright says, "I wanted to give, lend my tongue to the voiceless Negro boys." [19] In this light, the book becomes not just a story about one black man in the American South, but one about the universal black man of the South who lived through similar early experiences. He was writing, also, Wright says, to pass judgment on his childhood environment:

> That judgement was this: the environment the South creates is too small to nourish human beings, especially Negro human beings. Some may escape the general plights and grow up, but it is a matter of luck and I think it should be a matter of plan. It should be a matter of saving the citizens of our country for our country. [20]

That judgment, that social commentary, was met with the same critical acclaim as *Native Son*. Published in 1945, *Black Boy: A Record of Childhood and Youth* was assured success by becoming Wright's second book accepted for the Book of the Month Club. The book that was published, however, does not represent Wright's original intentions for the piece. On the advice of his editor, he broke the book into two distinct sections: The first represents his childhood and adolescence in the South (the *Black Boy* most students are familiar with today), and the second, titled *American Hunger,* recounts his experiences as a Communist in the North. With the latest 1998 printing of the work by Perennial Classics, the two books are published in one volume as *Black Boy (American Hunger): A Record of Childhood and Youth.*

Upon its original publication, *Black Boy* forced the American reader to consider the South from the black man's point of view for the first time. Wright's book, however, not only criticized the racist whites of the South, but also condemned blacks too readily submissive to Jim Crow laws, and all those who strove to make a "good Negro," an obedient, unquestioning black man, out of him. In doing so, Wright alienated himself from much of his past. Had the literary world not accepted him at this point, he would have been left without support from any quarter.

Black Boy was not an unqualified success. Black critic Ben Burns, for instance, referred to the book as "a sorry slander of Negroes generally," and said that Wright was not speaking for the universal black man of the South as he so claimed. "In *Black Boy,*" Burns continues, Wright "is again erring as he did in *Native Son* in his emphasis on the hopelessness of the Negro's lot, in his total failure to see that the clock of history is moving ahead, not backward." [21]

Despite this and similar criticism, *Black Boy* hit first place on the best-seller list on April 29, 1945, just one month after its publication, and remained there for a week. By the end of the year, it ranked fourth among all nonfiction sales; sales in translation were also brisk, finding an audience in Scandinavia, England, Brazil, and Palestine, among other countries. As a final testament to the book's success, *Black Boy* is widely studied in high school and college curricula today.

A NEW LIFE IN PARIS

In 1946, amid the great success of *Black Boy,* Wright and his family were invited on a month-long, all-expenses-paid trip to Paris by the French government. Wright, who for some time had been wanting to visit expatriate friend and writer Gertrude Stein in France, was overjoyed by the offer. In France he found that he was treated more as a celebrity and intellectual than he had been treated in the States.

Walker writes, "He was now an international figure welcomed on another continent and treated not merely as a worthy human being, but somebody special, illustrious, and held in reverence with no thought of condemnation because of race, color, or creed."[22] It was the kind of reception one imagines Wright had dreamed about when he wrote his first story in eighth grade; regrettably, he had to leave America to feel the kind of freedom he felt in Europe. In sum, he felt that Europeans were more cultured and, most importantly, more accepting of interracial couples. Wright had finally found a place where he truly felt at home. It is not surprising, therefore, that he and Ellen decided to move their family to Paris permanently in the summer of 1947.

Wright continued to expand both his career and his family while in Paris. His second daughter, Rachel, was born in January 1949, and he finished the screenplay of *Native Son* in the same year. Unable to interest Hollywood in the script without agreeing to unacceptable changes by producers, Wright and his partners sold the screenplay to European producers. Deciding to play the lead character, Bigger Thomas, himself, Wright remained closely connected with the production of the project, which was filmed in Chicago and Argentina.

Filming of *Native Son* wrapped up in June 1950 after a number of financial difficulties and other delays. The film finally opened in Buenos Aires in 1951, where it was met with triumphant reviews. Reaction was similar throughout other theaters in Europe. In America, however, it was a different story. American critics were unenthusiastic about both the acting and editing. Wright nonetheless defended the film, blaming its failure in America on censors who demanded thirty minutes of the film be cut before its premiere. Some theaters even refused to show the film at all.

THE LITERATURE OF WRIGHT'S LATER YEARS

Between 1953 and 1960, Wright continued to live and write in Paris. His first book published during this time (and first published since *Black Boy*) was *The Outsider*, appearing in 1953. Though it was sold as fiction, the book, like most of his work, was autobiographical in nature. In America, Wright's new book was widely reviewed, as American critics were eager to assess the effects of expatriation on his writing. Though the reviews were mixed, most were negative.

Always involved with another project, Wright did not let the negative reviews of *The Outsider* affect his work. In the same year of its release, he obtained a special visa to visit the Gold Coast of Ghana to gather material on Africans for his book *Black Power: A Record of Reactions in a Land of Pathos,* which was published in 1954. Another of Wright's novels, *Savage Holiday*, his only novel with all white characters, was published the same year. This novel was considered pulp fiction, published as a paperback, and did not receive serious attention from the academic or literary press. Wright's regular publishers rejected the book, and he worried that they would not accept any new work from him that did not explore issues of race.

As in the previous year, Wright did not let his literary success, or lack thereof, prevent him from moving forward with other plans. As before, he traveled, but this time to Spain with interest in another writing project. In 1955, Wright's travels took him to Indonesia, where he attended the Bandung Conference with numerous African and Asian leaders. The conference attendees discussed Third World problems and issues of racism and colonialism.

In 1956, Wright published his account of the conference, *The Color Curtain: A Report on the Bandung Conference.* His new book, *Pagan Spain*, based on his travels in Spain, appeared the same year as he began a lecture tour of several European countries. Neither work sold well, however, and both soon went out of print and remained so until the 1970s, when a resurgence of interest in Wright's work among American college students prompted reprints.

Wright published *White Man, Listen!,* a collection of lectures warning against continuing racism in America in 1957. The black press immediately praised the work, but the popular press criticized the work severely, calling him moralist and ungrateful. Whatever the critical response, Walker writes that the publication of this book represented the end of a cycle in Wright's life: "It represents his ten years of lecturing and traveling over Europe, Africa, and Asia. It also ends the ten years in Paris that have been overflowing with productivity. In ten years he had written nine books, traveled thousands of miles, and given dozens of lectures."[25]

THE FINAL YEARS

Although Wright wrote and published until his unexpected death, his last three years in Paris were not especially happy ones. Though they did not divorce, he and Ellen had been estranged since the filming of *Native Son*, and as Ellen had taken the girls to live in England to continue her career as a literary agent, he felt the marriage was essentially over. Additionally, Wright felt harassed by the American government's investigation of his former Communist associations, and in January 1959, his mother died in Mississippi. Wright himself suffered a bout of amoebic dysentery at the time, as well.

Richard Wright

Wright seemed to be suffering both financially and professionally. Since his later works did not sell well and his earlier, successful books were now out of print, he was not making much money from royalties. He was forced instead to take on small writing projects, such as writing reviews for jazz albums. The situation did not improve: Wright's feelings of rejection and discouragement intensified when he was unable to sell his novel *Island of Hallucinations*, which remains unpublished today.

Wright's last novel published in his lifetime represented his continuing move away from European issues and focus on American life. This book, *The Long Dream*, was published in 1958. It was the first in a projected trilogy about Mississippi that he hoped would rekindle critical interest in his work, but like much of his later work, the book received poor reviews and did not sell well. Likewise, a 1960 stage adaptation of *The Long Dream* opened on Broadway but closed in a week after poor reviews.

Wright's last literary activity was also in 1960, when he prepared more than eight hundred of his haiku for publication and began work on a new novel. *Eight Men*, a collection of short stories, was also ready for publication. It was published posthumously in 1961.

On November 28, 1960, Richard Wright died of a heart attack at age fifty-two. He was cremated with a copy of *Black Boy* on December 3 in Paris. The American press, though critical of his later work, mourned his untimely death and referred to him as a great American writer. Today, as readers discover Wright's novels, biographer Michel Fabre suggests that

> we must not forget that Richard Wright was attempting more than entertainment or even political enlightenment. Uncer-

tainly at times, but more often quite consciously, he was grappling with a definition of man. Although his solitary quest ended prematurely and did not allow him to find one, his achievement as a writer and a humanist makes him, in the Emersonian sense, a truly "representative man" of our time.[24]

NOTES

1. Michel Fabre, *The Unfinished Quest of Richard Wright.* New York: William Morrow, 1973, p. 10.
2. Addison Gayle, *Richard Wright: Ordeal of a Native Son.* New York: Anchor Press, 1990, pp. 9–10.
3. Quoted in Keneth Kinnamon, *The Emergence of Richard Wright.* Urbana: University of Illinois Press, 1972, p. 10.
4. Fabre, *The Unfinished Quest of Richard Wright,* p. 38.
5. Gayle, *Richard Wright,* p. 27.
6. Kinnamon, *The Emergence of Richard Wright,* p. 37.
7. Kinnamon, *The Emergence of Richard Wright,* p. 35.
8. Margaret Walker, *Richard Wright: Demonic Genius.* New York: Warner, 1988, p. 38.
9. Gayle, *Richard Wright,* p. 43.
10. Quoted in Fabre, *The Unfinished Quest of Richard Wright,* p. 65.
11. Quoted in Gayle, *Richard Wright,* p. 55.
12. Quoted in Gayle, *Richard Wright,* p. 89.
13. Kinnamon, *The Emergence of Richard Wright,* p. 51.
14. Fabre, *The Unfinished Quest of Richard Wright,* p. 97.
15. Quoted in Kinnamon, *The Emergence of Richard Wright,* p. 64.
16. Fabre, *The Unfinished Quest of Richard Wright,* p. 204.
17. Fabre, *The Unfinished Quest of Richard Wright,* p. 216.
18. Fabre, *The Unfinished Quest of Richard Wright,* p. 255.
19. Quoted in Fabre, *The Unfinished Quest of Richard Wright,* p. 252.
20. Quoted in Fabre, *The Unfinished Quest of Richard Wright,* p. 252.
21. Quoted in Fabre, *The Unfinished Quest of Richard Wright,* p. 280.
22. Walker, *Richard Wright,* pp. 198–99.
23. Walker, *Richard Wright,* p. 290.
24. Fabre, *The Unfinished Quest of Richard Wright,* p. 531.

CHAPTER 1

Structure and Style in *Black Boy*

READINGS ON
BLACK BOY

Richard Wright's *Black Boy:* A Twentieth-Century Slave Narrative

Sidonie Ann Smith

Literary scholar and author Sidonie Ann Smith explores how Wright's early home life depicted in *Black Boy* offers no forms of self-fulfillment and creativity, which fuels his frustration and rebellion against those at home. As the autobiography progresses, it becomes evident that this early unrest is symbolic of later social rebellion against the restrictions of the white society Wright is not allowed to enter. His only chance at self-actualization is through his energy and creativity as a writer, the pen his weapon against a society of inequality and injustice.

Prior to the recognition of such late nineteenth century Black American writers as Paul Laurence Dunbar and Charles Chesnutt, the most widely known black literary form was the personal narrative of the escaped slave or freedman known as the slave narrative. Stripped brutally of traditional means through which to derive a sense of identity, denied access to the study of letters, alienated from American society, the black slave had only himself to rely on for self-discovery and self-fulfillment. His own life story became a natural medium of such an expression. The controlling theme of these narratives, under which all other themes are subsumed, is the "freeing" of an authentic and fully human identity from the chains of the less-than-human identity forced upon the slave by American society. The slave narrator was the rebel who refused to choose either of two other responses which he witnessed all around him: the acceptance of the fate of oppression and the apparent acquiescence to it through the conscious masking of true feelings.

Excerpted from Sidonie Ann Smith, "Richard Wright's *Black Boy:* The Creative Impulse as Rebellion," *The Southern Literary Journal,* vol. 5, no. 1 (1972). Copyright © 1972 by the University of North Carolina Press. Used by permission of the publisher.

With the Civil War the slave narrative as such disappeared. But the slave system had merely been replaced by the caste system which perpetuated the imprisonment of the black American in the stereotypes of white America and thus his condemnation to invisibility. As a result, the literature of the black American by and large continues to be a personal literature, indeed, a modern version of the slave narrative, describing the quest of the black self for the "promised land" of a free identity.

In his autobiography, *Black Boy*, Richard Wright captured one of the most powerfully moving personal narratives of this very journey. Young Wright, living in the South in the first decades of the twentieth century where disenfranchisement, segregation, and racial subordination comprised the terms of existence, comes to recognize fully his imprisonment within Southern society. His impulse is to rebel openly, but to do so is to risk death. Yet Richard recognizes an even greater risk than death. To accept—or even appear to accept—the servility the South demands of him is to invite psychological suicide. Richard, who finds it impossible to accept or to mask the rebellion against this fate, ultimately chooses open rebellion. Thus, for Wright, the autobiographer, warfare—between his essential self and his environment—becomes the basic metaphor for depicting his struggle from childhood innocence to self-awareness. . . .

A SYMBOLIC GESTURE

His domestic environment oppressively denies Richard natural means for self-fulfillment. That the source of this deprivation should be the "old, white, wrinkled, grim face" of his grandmother is doubly significant: first, the feelings of repression and fear are symbolically linked to "whiteness"; second, literally and metaphorically, "black" becomes "white," rendering both "colors" potentially oppressive.

Richard, deprived of the normal outlets for his creative energies—running, playing, shouting, seeks an alternate form of self-affirmation. . . . His imaginative curiosity combines with his childhood frustration to find another outlet, the destructive act of burning the curtains which he has been forbidden to touch. Putting the torch to them is a means of acting out his rebellion against his oppressive domestic environment. This act of domestic rebellion is the symbolic precursor of his larger social rebellion, for the curtains are "fluffy white." In addition, they cover the windows, thereby keeping out the sun, and, in this way, symbolize the restrictions of white society which he is forbidden to "touch," to challenge. Herein lies the beginning of Richard's quest for self-actualization through rebellion. The curiosity and unfocused energy which propel this primal event, when informed by knowledge and sharpened by later suffering, become the creativity of the writer, ultimately the most powerful "weapon" in his arsenal of self-defense.

Richard's act of rebellion ends in total destruction of his domestic environment as his later rebellion is to threaten the status quo of the larger Southern environment. And from this destruction he now must and later will have to flee. Afraid of being punished, he escapes beneath the burning house only to be dragged out to suffer the punitive wrath of his mother. . . .

All throughout childhood, the family's protective instincts continue to terrify Richard who nevertheless challenges them repeatedly. In response the family resorts to beatings which Richard then refuses to suffer silently because he knows them to be unjustified. They are, rather, beatings that reflect the frustrations of the system. They are an act of love, but a distorted act of love: its intent is protection, its manner violence, its result destruction of personality. . . .

These violent encounters with his family are microcosmic reflections of his violent encounters with society at large. For the white bags simultaneously symbolize white society which, in response to his act of rebellion, seeks to drown him in the terrible liquid of nonentity and thereby wash away his imagination and individuality. Later, after his uncle is killed by a white mob, Richard, his mother, and aunt must flee secretly at night. Wright explains:

> Uncle Hoskins had simply been plucked from our midst and we, figuratively, had fallen on our faces to avoid looking into that white-hot face of terror that we knew loomed somewhere above us. This was as close as white terror had ever come to me and my mind reeled. Why had we not fought back, I asked my mother, and the fear that was in her made her slap me into silence.

His reaction . . . is terror and fear and a subsequent need to rebel against both white and black society. Significantly his mother slaps him out of fear when he asks, "Why had we not fought back." Fear—violence—counter-violence is an established pattern of behavior in Richard's life. His world becomes a cosmos of violence and repressive "love" as the black and white communities combine to demand a denial of self to which he cannot submit, against which he must rebel.

A REBEL IN THE MAKING

Richard, like the slave narrator, is imprisoned by the exigencies of survival in Southern society. Moreover, like the slave narrator, he is alone, a virtual orphan who must discover his own way to the "promised land" of self-actualization, for first his father and eventually his mother desert him. Early memories of his father, like the other early memories, abound in repression and violence:

> He became important and forbidding to me only when I learned that I could not make noise when he was asleep in the daytime. He was the lawgiver in our family and I never laughed in his presence. . . . He was always a stranger to me, always somehow alien and remote.

As a lawgiver Richard's father becomes an oppressor who controls rather than guides, an oppressor against whom he must rebel. When Richard and his brother bring home a stray cat, his father's response is emotionally violent: "'Kill that damn thing! . . . Do anything, but get it away from here!'" Richard does precisely this. When his mother reports this to this father, Richard taunts him: "'You told me to kill im.'" In this way, Richard defies his father's power and authority and thus triumphs over him. When soon after , his father leaves and hunger becomes a way of life, Richard's concept of "father" and "hunger" merge: "As the days slid past the image of my father became associated with my pangs of hunger, and whenever I felt hunger I thought of him with a deep biological bitterness."

Paradoxically, it is Richard's mother who temporarily becomes his guide, teaching him the necessary lesson of self-defense when she refuses to protect him from a gang of youths who, having once succeeded in stealing his grocery money, await him again. . . . Superficially this act seems to contradict her earlier violent response to his self-assertion. In the earlier instance, she, as a representative of the community, punishes him for this violent self-assertiveness: in the latter instance, she forces him to respond violently towards others. But actually both these lessons are lessons in

self-defense: the first is a lesson that is necessary for survival in white society; the second, a lesson necessary for survival in black. Richard is, at this time, forced literally to fight
in order to survive the life of the streets. As he matures, the
value of self-assertion through physical warfare will find
new avenues of expression in psychological and verbal warfare.

When his mother finally succumbs to permanent illness
and disability, Richard is deprived of his last familial source
of strength. Her illness was to affect him profoundly:

> My mother's suffering grew into a symbol in mind, gathering
> to itself all the poverty, the ignorance, the helplessness; the
> painful, baffling, hunger-ridden days and hours; the restless
> moving, the futile seeking, the uncertainty, the fear, the
> dread; the meaningless pain and the endless suffering. Her
> life set the emotional tone of my life, colored the men and
> women I was to meet in the future, conditioned my relation
> to events that had not yet happened, determined my attitude
> to situations and circumstances I had yet to face. A somber-
> ness of spirit that I was never to lose settled over me during
> the slow years of my mother's unrelieved suffering, a
> somberness that was to make me stand apart and look upon
> excessive joy with suspicion, that was to make me self-
> conscious, that was to make me keep forever on the move, as
> though to escape a nameless fate seeking to overtake me.

The older autobiographer looks back upon this loss, assigning to it in retrospect the meaning that it came to hold for his
later life. For the more modern slave narrator, the dogs of the
overseer still pursue, though they have assumed the qualities of a more general "fate"—one that has its origin in the
bitter experience of childhood.

As a result of this bitter experience the twelve-year-old
boy forms a "conception of life": "the meaning of living came
only when one was struggling to wring a meaning out of
meaningless suffering." This struggle is the struggle of the
rebel who refuses to acquiesce in the conspiracy of this
black family community, a microcosm of the community at
large, to force him to deny his individuality and is, therefore,
alienated completely from anything but his own self-
consciousness. Richard recognizes that the separation he
feels is deadly when he says of himself at the age of fifteen:

> In me was shaping a yearning for a kind of consciousness, a
> mode of being that the way of life around me had said could
> not be, must not be, and upon which the penalty of death had
> been placed.

REJECTING INVISIBILITY

His longing to be an authentic self struggles against society's demand that he be a "nigger." The struggle sharpens his anger toward a hostile world as it taxes his inner resolve to overcome that world.

Richard shrinks from the two frequently travelled roads to survival for a black in Southern society. There is the rigid, stifling religion of his grandmother, Aunt Aggie, and his mother, which encourages resignation to the world by preaching that there will be revenge enough in inheriting the next. Or, there is the masking of Griggs and Shorty which provides the limited psychological revenge of conscious deception. . . . The Christian tenet of long-suffering and Grigg's tactic of masking true feelings repel Richard, however much they insure survival. Religion, since it denies the self, applauds the selfless and promises heavenly fulfillment, devalues the needs of oppressed blacks in the here-and-now and counsels them to be content with their social position. Masking also denies legitimate self-assertion, since the real responses of the self must consciously be sacrificed to the mask. Sometimes it even demands self-degradation, as when Shorty allows a white man to kick him in order to get twenty-five cents for lunch. Both options spell mere survival. In the one instance, a wall of other-worldliness and, in the other, a wall of disguise protect the individual from destruction but keep him from attacking the sources of his oppression. So imprisoned, the individual is condemned to invisibility.

The curse of invisibility is to be treated as an object, a state of being symbolized by two names—"nigger" and "boy." The former is symbolic of the denial of individuality, the latter the denial of manhood. These two names function, as do the methods of survival, to keep Richard physically and psychologically in his invisible "place." They are used by white society, but, in a more immediate way, they are used by black society so that he will survive in a white society. (When his family chastises him for some breach of social action, they call him "nigger.")

Against his will, Richard temporarily succumbs to these social identities in order to survive: he lies, steals, wears the mask of fawning ingratiation. The price, of course, is a half-life. As he puts it:

> I had been what my surroundings had demanded, what my family—conforming to the dictates of the whites above them— had exacted of me, and what the whites had said that I must

be. Never being fully able to be myself, I had slowly learned
that the South could recognize but a part of a man.

But, ultimately, he chooses to reject this social mask of infe-
riority and invisibility and, in doing so, becomes a full-
fledged rebel. Until this point his only weapon against this
stigmatizing invisibility has been violence against his immediate family rather than society at large. But it is the
"word" which will ultimately become the weapon, the
sword, with which he attacks society and liberates his own
essential self.

A COURTSHIP WITH WORDS

At an early age Richard perceives the power of words; his
early experiences with them are violently punitive. There
are the words he learns at school and scrawls on neighborhood walls, which his mother threateningly makes him
wash off completely. Later, after the story of *Bluebeard and
His Seven Wives* elicits a "total emotional response" from
him, he tries to read by himself. . . . Without understanding
the meaning of words, Richard responds to their evocative
power. Then one evening, as his grandmother washes him,
"words—words whose meaning I did not fully know—had
slipped out of my mouth." He had asked his grandmother to
kiss him "back there," and for this he suffers the wrath of the
entire family. Feeling no guilt, unable to comprehend why
he should be punished, Richard only recognizes the effect of
those words upon others, a power which fascinates him:

> The tremendous upheaval that my words had caused made
> me know that there lay back of them much more than I could
> figure out, and I resolved that in the future I would learn the
> meaning of why they had beat and denounced me.

The courtship with words extends throughout his youth:
he reads everything he can find and even tries his hand at
short-story writing. The successful publication of one story,
however, does not gain him the praise he desires, but rather
chastisement and misunderstanding. Later he idealistically
decides upon a career in writing and shares his dream with
a new employer, whose reaction is significantly described as
an "assault" on his ego. She asks him why he is continuing
his education beyond the seventh grade: he answers that he
wants to become a writer.

"A what" she demanded.

"A writer," I mumbled.

"For what?"

"To write stories," I mumbled defensively.

"You'll never be a writer," she said. "Who on earth put such ideas into your nigger head?"

"Nobody," I said.

"I didn't think anybody ever would," she declared indignantly.

As I walked around her house to the street, I knew that I would not go back. The woman had assaulted my ego; she had assumed that she knew my place in life, what I felt, what I ought to be, and I resented it with all my heart. Perhaps she was right; perhaps I would never be a writer, but I did not want her to say so.

Writing, for a black, lay beyond the structure of socially acceptable possibilities in the South and thus is linked with self-assertion, individuality, manhood, and, by association, with rebellion. His family's negative response to his successful attempt at short-story writing and the white woman's incredulous response both show a recognition of the rebellion inherent in such a dream.

WRITING TOWARDS A VISIBLE SELF

Richard comes to appreciate this association fully when he reads [satirist and critic] H.L. Mencken, a decisive step in his development: he comes to recognize the militancy and potential violence of words, a violence he has already experienced emotionally but not intellectually. . . .

Wright's portrait of Mencken is significant: "I pictured the man as a raging demon, slashing with his pen." The pen becomes the most effective weapon of warfare and, for the imagination, becomes the equivalent of physical violence. This initiation into the weaponry of words leads him on to more and more writers who awaken him to the reality of the world outside the South. He finds in writers the attitudes towards life he has harbored alone within himself.

Wright will imitate Mencken when, in his later writing, he uses the pen as weapon, the word as ammunition for protesting the life of the black American. . . .

Wright's autobiography is essentially a twentieth-century version of the earlier slave narrative, explicitly and implicitly echoing its themes. Emancipation has not brought freedom to the South even half a century after its inception: the South remains a slave plantation where Richard is still imprisoned in an oppressive, less-than-human social identity.

There, he is—and will ever remain—a "nigger" and a "boy." Thus, like the slave narrator's story, Wright's autobiography is the story of a self willing to rebel to the point of annihilation in order to remain inviolate. Richard's longing for visible selfhood rather than deceptive invisibility makes subservience to the racial norms of the South impossible for him. He must flee to escape emasculation. His running is a positive act for it is potentially redemptive. And it has direction: the North beckons with possibility. The last pages of *Black Boy* testify to his hope, like that of the slave narrator before him, that a "home" and a "better day" await him in the North.

His journey, however, is not informed by unqualified hope. He realizes that he will always carry the South with him, for he is its child. But he envisions himself as a hopeful "experiment.". . . Moreover, he knows that he is running *away* from the South as much as he is running *to* the North. The autobiography does not conclude with Wright's having achieved a new identity, but rather with his breaking away from his past and hoping for a rebirth, a blooming, into a new, more legitimate self. That the hope ultimately shatters and the new identity eludes him in the North is another story, the story narrated in the parts of *Black Boy* that have remained unpublished, the story implicit in Wright's eventual expatriation to France.

Narrative Structure of *Black Boy*

John O. Hodges

Professor of American and religious studies at the University of Tennessee, John O. Hodges demonstrates two of Wright's core objectives in the narrative structure of *Black Boy:* to report his own experience and to expose the brutality and insensitivity of the South. To accomplish this task, Wright structures his narrative around the perspectives of two narrators: the boy whose life symbolizes the lives of many black youths of Wright's time, and the adult author who interprets his experiences.

As the story of a boy's journey from ignorance to experience, *Black Boy* possesses significant features of the classical *Bildungsroman*, a work which recounts a young man's education or character formation. According to Roy Pascal in his book *The German Novel*, the *Bildungsroman* is the "story of the formation of a character up to the moment when he ceases to be self-centered and becomes society-centered, thus beginning to form his true Self." And *Black Boy* is the story of a boy whose selfhood must be forged in the crucible of a hostile society which is determined to suppress any positive assertion of personhood. Since Richard is interested in pursuing a literary career, the restrictions which his society places upon him become all the more serious. *Black Boy*, then, like other exemplary works in the genre . . . depicts the arduous pilgrimage of the embattled artist in a restrictive environment. . . .

But while *Black Boy* adheres to the structural design of the *Bildungsroman*, the book goes significantly beyond the genre's usual theme of a boy's awakening self-consciousness as he apprehends the mysteries of the world about him. In *Black Boy*, Richard must win self-knowledge in a society

Excerpted from John O. Hodges, "An Apprenticeship to Life and Art: Narrative Design in Wright's *Black Boy*," *CLA Journal*, vol. 28 (June 1985), pp. 415–33. Reprinted by permission of the publisher.

that is not only repressive and restrictive but profoundly antagonistic as well. And this antagonism is experienced not
only in his effort to become a writer but at every level, even
at the fundamental level of human survival itself. There is
also, in *Black Boy*, a fraternal dimension unlike anything we
find in the typical *Bildungsroman*. For Wright attempts to
call attention not only to his own difficult journey but to that
of other black youths who attempted to take hold of the
meaning of their lives in the hostile atmosphere of the deep
American South of a few generations ago.

In the course of a radio interview in the spring of 1945,
Wright set forth very candidly what had been his basic intention in *Black Boy*:

> I wrote the book to tell a series of incidents strung through
> my childhood, but the main desire was to render a judgment
> on my environment because I felt the necessity to. That judg-
> ment was this: the environment the South creates is too small
> to nourish human beings.... I wanted to lend, give my
> tongue to the voiceless Negro boys.

Indeed, the self-portrait which emerges is of one whose experience embraced the worst hardships suffered by blacks under
the Southern caste system. And, inevitably, his purpose required him to suppress certain details of his life and to exag-
gerate others, in order that the narrative design might stress
the ordeals experienced by a typical Southern black. His account, though autobiographical, "would be more than that; he
would use himself as a symbol of all the brutality wreaked
upon the black man by the Southern environment...."

The writing of *Black Boy*, therefore, was meant to serve at
least two purposes: that of enabling Wright to retrace his
steps in order to understand himself and to understand
where he stood in relationship to the black community; and
that of creating a platform from which a judgment might be
pronounced on the Southern white society which blighted
the hopes and aspirations of its black youth. My intention
here is to demonstrate how Wright, by carefully designing
and narrating the story of his life, attempts to accomplish simultaneously these distinct objectives within the narrative
structure of his autobiography.

Wright's two-fold objective of reporting on his own experience and of exposing the brutality and insensitivity of the
South required him to adopt a rather elaborate narrative
strategy. He had to present the story from the perspective of

an average black boy victimized and brutalized by his experiences in the South, while at the same time accounting for the fact that those very experiences, though daunting for so many, had actually goaded him toward significant achievement. Furthermore, he had to devise a method whereby he could criticize what he considered to be shortcomings in his own people, while also holding the white South responsible for those shortcomings. Wright's intention required him to exploit fully the tension between past and present, between the boy who experiences and the mature author who interprets.

A NOVEL IN TWO VOICES

Therefore, although the account appears to be presented from the perspective of a first-person narrator, we detect two distinct voices, two "I's." On the one hand, we have the "I" of the narrative present where the account is presented from the point of view of the boy's own developing consciousness as he confronts each new experience. On the other hand, we have the "I" of the writer as he imposes his present state of consciousness on the events of the narrative. This latter type of "telling" narration (in Wayne Booth's sense) makes it possible for the writer to interpret and even to criticize the protagonist's actions from the standpoint of his (the writer's) present knowledge of the outcome of those events. Furthermore, the "intrusive" narrator attempts to convince his audience of the soundness or unsoundness of the boy's actions.

Indeed, even when the narration is filtered through the consciousness of the boy, we recognize the author's hand, for young Richard is made to speak words and to handle metaphors and symbols which he, because of his immaturity, could not possibly have understood. So in this sense, too, the protagonist is made to speak for the author. Yet this type of narration succeeds in ways that the intrusive narration does not, because once the author has prepared the script for the ensuing action, he appears to withdraw from the scene and allows the hero to occupy the center of the stage. From this point of view the audience is able to judge firsthand not only the conduct of the protagonist who speaks the language and attempts to manipulate the symbols of the author, but also the attitude of the author toward his protagonist. And since the protagonist speaks for the author, we are actually determining the author's *present* attitude toward his past.

Perhaps one of the most effective means of charting Richard's growth of consciousness is through the author's use of a "naive" hero, a technique which is commonly associated with the *Bildungsroman* convention. It is only through incessant probing and at the expense of great pain and suffering that the boy begins to unlock the various secrets and mysteries of the adult world. After Granny gives him his bath, he tells her to "kiss back there," and his parents give him a stern beating. Concerning this he writes: "[I]n the future I would learn the meaning of why they had beat and denounced me." And, in general, he notices that his mother becomes extremely irritated whenever he inquires about the relationship between blacks and whites. When he asks her why the family chose not to fight back when Uncle Hoskins was killed, she immediately slaps him. Or again, when he sees a black chain gang being driven by white guards (which he at first takes to be a herd of elephants), he asks his mother whether the white men ever wore stripes, to which she reluctantly replies, "sometimes," though she herself never saw any. Thus, for young Richard, "[t]he days and hours began to speak with a clearer tongue. Each new experience had a sharp meaning of its own."

The primary role of the "naive" hero, however, is to call into question those injustices which blacks and whites, because of habit and custom, dismiss all too perfunctorily. In short, the boy, in wearing the mask of the author, forces those about him—and Wright's readers as well—to examine the deeper implications of their actions. The boy, perhaps because he is ignorant of the customs of Jim Crow, is free of the bigotry and prejudice that hinder blacks and whites from achieving any stable relationships in the South. He exhibits, furthermore, a higher moral sense and a greater sensitivity than do the more mature individuals about him, and he thus becomes an adequate "voice" for revealing the hypocrisy and ruthlessness of the South during Wright's youth.

Dialogue is yet another form of narration which enables us to observe the drama of selfhood as it unfolds in the autobiography. As the youth converses with others, both blacks and whites, who are more mature and sophisticated than he, we learn much about his personality and developing consciousness, especially about how he sees himself in relation to these individuals. Here again, however, as with the other forms of narration, the portrait that we have is one which is determined more by the author's present attitudes and experiences than by any actual events in his past. Since he cannot possibly recall with absolute exactness the various exchanges he has had with others, he must search his present storehouse of words, images, and symbols for suitable metaphors of those past experiences. The author, therefore, is "free" to recreate the dialogues in a manner which best accords with his own general purpose and intention. And it is by way of Wright's effort to give his narrative a true structure—that is, to make it stand for more than a mere chronology of the major events of his life—that the various modes of narration come to play such an important role.

The whole narrative design of the book functions in conjunction with elements of structure and theme in order to produce the total effect of a boy's difficult journey from innocence to experience. It is to a closer examination of the process of this boy's education that we must now turn.

THE NAIVE NARRATOR BEGINS THE TALE

Wright recounts the crucial experiences of his youth with extraordinary poignancy, and one feels that it is his hope to make his readers at once conscious of and also in some sense prepared to take responsibility for the anguish which he and other black boys experienced in the South of his day. The boy's awakening self-consciousness evolves in stages which correspond to the three sectors of society through which he successively moves: his own household, the black community, and the larger white world. Richard's understanding of himself and of the world he inhabits increases with each new *rite de passage*, so that once he has encountered the whole of Southern life, he has a clearer knowledge of who he is and of the future course his life must take.

The narrator begins the story of his life not with its beginning but with those "four-year-old days," the time when he first becomes conscious of the fear, hunger, and violence that are to plague him throughout his childhood. Wright's decision not to recount the circumstances of his birth betrays his intention to thrust young Richard's developing selfhood immediately into the center of the design.

The opening lines establish the tone of fear and despair which pervades the entire narrative. While the atmosphere of anxiety and dread stems at this point from within

Richard's own household, we get the impression that it only presages the larger insecurities which he is to encounter in the outside world. Richard seems to fear his grandmother, for instance, not so much because she is a stern taskmaster, but because she is, for all intents and purposes, white: "I was dreaming of running and playing and shouting but the vivid image of Granny's old, white, wrinkled, grim face framed by a halo of tumbling black hair, lying upon a huge feather pillow, made me afraid." Later on in his recital the narrator confides to us that, indeed, his "grandmother was as nearly white as a Negro can get without being white, which means that she was white." The color white, then, already begins to take on a decidedly sinister aspect, and, though Richard appears unaware of the fact at this point, it seems to have been a color which in his experience was regularly associated with restrictiveness. . . .

The whippings this boy receives, though no doubt excessive, are meant to curb that natural curiosity which, outside the home, could result in his death. Furthermore, he is warned against asking too many questions regarding the nature of the relationship between blacks and whites. When he learns of a white man having beaten a black boy, Richard does not understand, for, as he reasons, "a paternal right is the only right that a man has to beat a child." And though his mother refuses to answer forthrightly all of the boy's queries—as he must be spared the bitter realities of his existence—the questions he raises are penetrating ones that are meant to disturb our consciences.

Richard's father is also a source of fear and anxiety. The narrator recalls: "He was the lawgiver in our family and I never laughed in his presence." Though his father's disappearance early on in his life means that he can enjoy a relatively greater degree of freedom, unfortunately it also means greater hardship for the family. There is, for example, never enough food in the house. Indeed, he recalls: "Hunger was with us always. . . . As the days slid past the image of my father became associated with my pangs of hunger, and whenever I felt hunger I thought of him with a deep biological bitterness."

Although the narrator insists that he has since forgiven his father, they were "forever strangers, speaking a different language, living on vastly different planes of reality. . . ." While he himself had gone on to achieve some measure of success, his father remained "imprisoned by the slow flow of the seasons, by wind and rain and sun." Wright's judgment is indeed a harsh one, as he seems to attack his father for a lack of resourcefulness and courage because he permitted himself to be defeated by the pressures of the Southern experience. Moreover, having by the end of the opening chapter been accounted a failure, the elder Wright from this point on plays no part in the narrative, as though the son had chosen simply to expel him from the circle of his attention.

LEARNING TO SURVIVE

Without the spiritual support of a father, Richard frequents bars where he learns to speak obscenities even before he can read. And worse, he declares, "I was a drunkard in my sixth year before I had begun school." His mother now not only has to provide the economic support for the family, but she has the added responsibility of teaching the boy those methods of survival on which his life depends. It is she, for example, who teaches him to fight back when he is attacked by a gang of boys in Memphis who threaten to take the money he has been given to purchase groceries.

Besides learning how to survive in the streets and taverns of Memphis, Richard has also to learn how to deal with the bitter friction which exists between the two races. While he had witnessed the beating of a black boy by a white policeman and had heard stories of violent encounters between blacks and whites, it is not until he visits Granny in Jackson that he begins to understand the seriousness of the hostility which exists between "the two races who lived side by side but never touched, it seemed, except in violence." Significantly, his first real experience of violence (apart from the harsh punishment he receives at the hands of his parents) is a vicarious one which he receives as Ella, a school teacher who rents a room in Granny's house, reads him one of her stories entitled "Bluebeard and His Seven Wives.". . . This is a most crucial passage in the narrative, for it gives us the first real indication of the boy's interest in imaginative literature. Moreover, the violence which lay at the heart of the story mirrored the violence in his own life and gave it a deeper meaning:

> I hungered for the sharp, frightening, breath-taking, almost painful excitement that the story had given me, and I vowed that as soon as I was old enough I would buy all the novels

there were and read them to feed that thirst for violence that was in me, for intrigue, for plotting, for secrecy, for bloody murders. . . . They could not have known that Ella's whispered story of deception and murder had been the first experience in my life that had elicited from me at total emotional response.

He soon was to see the bloody drama Bluebeard acted out in real life. While visiting his Aunt Maggie, Richard learns that Uncle Hoskins has been killed by whites who had long coveted his flourishing liquor business. On another occasion Matthews, Aunt Maggie's new husband, bludgeons the white girl who witnessed him stealing some money from her house and then sets the house on fire, leaving the girl to perish in the flames. There is also the violence which resulted at the close of the First World War when racial conflict permeated the South. The narrator recalls, "Though I did not witness any of it, I could not have been more thoroughly affected by it if I had participated directly in the clash."

THE MATURE NARRATOR REFLECTS ON SUFFERING

The violence, the fear, the hunger—the basic realities of this boy's childhood—seemed to be symbolized in his mother's suffering, to the extent that, as he says, "her life set the emotional tone of my life." The suffering he experienced in his youth, he suggests, brought him to a deeper sense of communal responsibility:

> The spirit I had caught gave me insight into the sufferings of others, made me gravitate toward those whose feelings were like my own, made me sit for hours while others told me of their lives, made me strangely tender and cruel, violent and peaceful.

The entire passage here is clearly informed by a wider knowledge and consciousness than that of a twelve-year-old boy. The mature writer temporarily enters his narrative in order to interpret the experiences thus far recorded and to show their relevance to his general growth and development. By reflecting on his past in such a manner, he discovers himself in the present and justifies his present conduct and ideology in those past experiences.

When his mother's deteriorating health makes it necessary that he find some kind of employment, he has to confront that hatred and fear which he has seen debase and even destroy other blacks. So as the narrator moves from the relatively safe confines of his home and the black community into the white world, . . . Richard wonders if his experiences at home and in his community have adequately prepared him for the hazards of the white world: "What would happen now that I would be among white people for hours at a stretch? Would they hit me? Curse me?"

At his first job where he was to earn just two dollars a week, the white woman engages him in a significant dialogue:

> "Now, boy, I want to ask you one question and I want you to tell me the truth," she said.
> "Yes, ma'am." I said, all attention.
> "Do you steal?" she asked seriously.
> I bust into a laugh, then checked myself.
> "What's so damn funny about that?" she asked.
> "Lady, if I was a thief, I'd never tell anybody."
> "What do you mean?" she blazed with a red face.
> I had made a mistake during my first five minutes in the white world. I hung my head.

The two characters here are acting out a typical scene between blacks and whites in the South. But it is clearly a little drama in which the two parties are both to be viewed as victims of the Southern caste system—the one because she has been trained only to echo conventional clichés about blacks, the other because, while conscious of the woman's ignorance, he must learn to disguise his true feelings, to dissemble and deny his own worth and dignity. For Richard, however, this feigning in the presence of whites proves to be an art most difficult to master. . . . And though Richard can never be as submissive as the other black boys, he too would soon learn that, in the South, "acting" is often the only weapon of survival. "The safety of my life," he tells us later on in his account, "depended on how well I concealed from all whites what I felt."

REJECTING THE SUBMISSIVE ROLE

As he moves about from one job to the next, he slowly learns how a black boy is required to reckon with Jim Crow. At one job the woman is surprised that he, a black boy from Mississippi, does not know how to milk a cow; at another he is bitten by a dog only to be told by the foreman that he has "never seen a dog yet that could hurt a nigger"; at still another, he has what is nearly a violent confrontation with two white employees who are infuriated by his eagerness to learn a "white man's trade." Perhaps his most galling experience occurs while working as a hallboy in the Jackson hotel where, earlier, Ned's brother had been killed. While walking toward his home with one of the black maids headed in the same general direction, he becomes spell-bound at seeing a white night watchman playfully slap her on the buttocks, but becomes even more astonished at the casualness with which the girl herself seems to treat the matter. He learns later that his brief moment of shock over such a routine act had almost cost him his life. And later, as a bellboy in the same hotel, he has to learn to avert his eyes from the white prostitutes who regularly lie nude across their beds. Reflecting on this, he writes: "Our presence awoke in them no sense of shame whatever, for we blacks were not considered human anyway.

In all these experiences, Richard notes a concerted effort on the part of whites—and given tacit approval by the blacks themselves—to consign him to a subservient role and to deny him that freedom of the will apart from which the creative mind cannot develop and flourish. In this context, the exchange with his first white employer takes on added significance. . . . Richard declares what we have suspected all along, that he is interested in a literary career. The disclosure itself is not surprising, but the manner and circumstance under which it is made have significant implications. The woman was merely voicing a sentiment held by the majority of whites in the South: that there were certain areas of human endeavor beyond the range of possibility for any blacks. More tragic still, his own family and members of the black community seemed to have conspired with the white world in its effort to smother any capacity he might have for a literary career. Granny did not want Ella to read him her stories because they were "the devil's works." His own story, "The Voodoo of Hell's Half-Acre," only served further to alienate him from his schoolmates and family: "From no quarter, with the exception of the Negro newspaper editor, had there come a single encouraging word."

From this point on in the narrative the restrictions which Richard faces are those associated with his quest to become a writer. He dreams of going to the North, which is for him a place of freedom where he might, in his words, "do something to redeem my being alive.". . .

THE AUTHOR EMERGES

By way of stealing goods and reselling them—an act which, where any black person was concerned, was morally acceptable to the South—he finally acquires enough money to leave for Memphis. Although his experience in Memphis is no happier, at least here he is able to satisfy his childhood hunger for reading by devising a scheme for getting books from the public library—which is generally off-limits to any blacks. Whites had often sent him to the library to get books for themselves. So he wonders how he might get books on his own. Having persuaded one of the more liberal whites to lend him his card, he forges the note: "Let this nigger boy have some books by H.L. Mencken." In this manner, he is able to read a body of literature ranging all the way from Anatole France to Sinclair Lewis. What interests Richard most about the writers he encounters in this way is their ability to use language as a weapon for striking out against the ills plaguing society. These writers were, in the boy's mind, "fighting with words." "I derived from these novels," he says, "nothing less than a sense of life itself. All my life had shaped me for the realism, the naturalism of the modern novel, and I could not read enough of them." He says further: "It had been my accidental reading of fiction and literary criticism that had evoked in me a glimpse of life's possibilities."

The language of this entire concluding section of *Black Boy* is not that of the boy but that of the mature man, not that of the aspiring writer but that of the accomplished author. As the narrative ends before Richard's nineteenth year, the author, for the sake of his readers, has to furnish such information as will enable us to see the relationship between the experiences of the boy and the writer he finally became. But it is, in fact, a difficult connection for us to make, since Wright himself at the time had no clear conception of his future lifework. His random reading, impressive in its range as it was for a boy in his circumstances, afforded him no clear vision of the possibility of his electing a literary vocation. Indeed, it was only after he had become sufficiently removed from the galling experiences of his boyhood and had gained some understanding of the writer's craft that he could impose some pattern on the raw experiences of his past and transmute them into literary art. In this respect, then, *Black Boy* clearly points to *American Hunger*, which details his struggles to become a writer in Chicago. The book, which appeared in 1977, was originally designed to be published along with *Black Boy* as a single work. But at the behest of his publisher, Wright agreed to have the section treating his experiences in the North issued later as a separate volume, for both men realized that though this work offered important insights into Wright's later years, it had neither the scope nor the intensity of the volume which chronicled his years in the South.

So *Black Boy* stands as Wright's major achievement in the mode of autobiographical literature, and it presents the important events comprising his apprenticeship to life and to art. The violence, the fear, the hunger, and all such negative experiences would in time provide him with rich resources for his art, for "wringing meaning out of meaningless suffering."

Richard Wright Sings the Blues

Ralph Ellison

Respected author of *The Invisible Man* and professor emeritus at New York University, Ralph Ellison explains that *Black Boy* is influenced in part by the blues, an autobiographical narrative of personal catastrophe expressed through lyricism. Like the musical blues, Wright's story offers no solutions for African Americans; rather, it forces them, and others, to confront the world and evaluate it honestly.

What in the tradition of literary autobiography is it like, this work described as a "great American autobiography"? As a nonwhite intellectual's statement of his relationship to western culture, *Black Boy* recalls the conflicting pattern of identification and rejection found in Nehru's *Toward Freedom*. In its use of fictional techniques, its concern with criminality (sin) and the artistic sensibility, and in its author's judgment and rejection of the narrow world of his origin, it recalls Joyce's rejection of Dublin in *A Portrait of the Artist*. And as a psychological document of life under oppressive conditions, it recalls *The House of the Dead*, Dostoievski's profound study of the humanity of Russian criminals. Such works were perhaps Wright's literary guides, aiding him to endow his life's incidents with communicable significance; providing him with ways of seeing, feeling, and describing his environment. These influences, however, were encountered only after these first years of Wright's life were past and were not part of the immediate folk culture into which he was born. In that culture the specific folk-art form which helped shape the writer's attitude towards his life and which embodied the impulse that contributes much to the quality and tone of his autobiography was the Negro blues. This would bear a word of explanation:

Excerpted from Ralph Ellison, "Richard Wright's Blues," *Antioch Review*, vol. 5, no. 2 (Summer 1945). Copyright © 1945 by the Antioch Review, Inc. Reprinted by permission of the editors.

The blues is an impulse to keep the painful details and episodes of a brutal experience alive in one's aching consciousness, to finger its jagged grain, and to transcend it, not by the consolation of philosophy, but by squeezing from it a near-tragic, near-comic lyricism. As a form, the blues is an autobiographical chronicle of personal catastrophe expressed lyrically. And certainly Wright's early childhood was crammed with catastrophic incidents. In a few short years his father deserted his mother, he knew intense hunger, he became a drunkard begging drinks from black stevedores in Memphis saloons; he had to flee Arkansas where an uncle was lynched; he was forced to live with a fanatically religious grandmother in an atmosphere of constant bickering; he was lodged in an orphan asylum; he observed the suffering of his mother who became a permanent invalid, while fighting off the blows of the poverty-stricken relatives with whom he had to live; he was cheated, beaten, and kicked off jobs by white employees who disliked his eagerness to learn a trade; and to these objective circumstances must be added the subjective fact that Wright, with his sensitivity, extreme shyness, and intelligence was a problem child who rejected his family and was by them rejected. . . .

THE BLUES IN *BLACK BOY*

Black Boy is filled with blues-tempered echoes of railroad trains, the names of southern towns and cities, estrangements, fights and flights, deaths and disappointments, charged with physical and spiritual hungers and pain. And like a blues sung by such an artist as Bessie Smith, its lyrical prose evokes the paradoxical, almost surreal image of a black boy singing lustily as he probes his own grievous wound. . . .

Let us close with one final word about the blues: Their attraction lies in this, that they at once express both the agony of life and the possibility of conquering it through sheer toughness of spirit. They fall short of tragedy only in that they provide no solution, offer no scapegoat but the self. Nowhere in America today is there social or political action based upon the solid realities of Negro life depicted in *Black Boy;* perhaps that is why, with its refusal to offer solutions, it is like the blues. Yet, in it thousands of Negroes will for the first time see their destiny in public print. Freed here of fear and the threat of violence, their lives have at last been organized, scaled down to possessable proportions. And in this lies Wright's most important achievement: he has converted the American Negro impulse towards self-annihilation and "going-under-ground" into a will to confront the world, to evaluate his experience honestly and throw his findings unashamedly into the guilty conscience of America.

Black Boy Is Incomplete Without *American Hunger*

Janice Thaddeus

Richard Wright scholar Janice Thaddeus of Barnard College argues that *Black Boy*, a truncated version of Wright's full autobiography, *American Hunger*, should be reissued in its entirety and without its revised six-page ending. The decision to publish *American Hunger* in separate parts masks Wright's original intent and suggests feelings of hope, when, in fact, he felt isolated in a world that lacked both conviction and order.

Black Boy's epigraph sets its theme, but that theme is para-doxical. Wright initiates his book with an unsettling quota-tion from Job: "They meet with darkness in the daytime / And they grope at noonday as in the night. . . ." Darkness and daytime, black and white, are insistent images throughout. Given the subject matter, this is an obvious choice, but Wright presents his oppositions with puzzling complexity. He mentions in passing in the opening paragraph that his grandmother is white, but it is not until fifty pages later that we discover that Granny was a slave, that she bears the name as well as the color of her white owner, that she does not know—or does not care to know—who her father was. If Granny is white, why is she black? The question is simple, but the answer is not, and Wright emphasizes this indefi-niteness. In many scenes, as Gayle Gaskill has shown, Wright deliberately reverses the usual connotations Western tradition has assigned to black and white—that black is al-ways bad and white good. . . . Throughout *Black Boy* Wright's imagery of black and white resists simple formulations. He has not shaped and tailored it to a simple, clear purpose.

Excerpted from Janice Thaddeus, "The Metamorphosis of Richard Wright's *Black Boy*," *American Literature*, vol. 52, no. 2 (May 1985). Copyright © 1985, Duke Univer-sity Press. Reprinted with permission from the publisher. (Footnotes in the original have been omitted in this reprint.)

The imagery of light and dark is similarly mutable. The South is dark, so dark that Wright frequently wonders over the fact that the sun is still shining. When he hears that an acquaintance has been lynched for presumably consorting with a white prostitute, it seems uncanny that life can continue: "I stood looking down the quiet, sun-filled street. Bob had been caught by the white death." Here, although the light is beautiful, whiteness means death. As readers, we recognize the reference to the black death, and are forced to the analogy that the animals carrying this plague are human. When Pease and Reynolds force Wright out of the optical shop where he had hoped to learn a trade to help people literally to improve their vision, he recounts: "I went into the sunshine and walked home like a blind man." The sun shines, but not for him. In ironic and various ways, then, aesthetically and thematically, the book fulfills its epigraph. The result, however, is anxiety, not resolution.

Black Boy is a violent book, but it has not been sufficiently noted that violence is always linked with its opposite, in a poised opposition resembling the metaphorical tension just discussed. Wright's experiences have made him "strangely tender and cruel, violent and peaceful." Besides the imagery mentioned above, Wright's chief word for this indefinable yearning is hunger. The word and the fact of hunger recur like drumbeats throughout the book, an insistent refrain. Wright never has enough to eat: he steals food even when there is plenty; he receives an orange for Christmas and eats it with preternatural care; he fills his aching stomach with water; he is too thin to pass the postal examination. The hunger is both "bodily and spiritual" and the spiritual hunger is as insistent as its bodily counterpart. The entire book is strung between hunger and satisfaction, as well as light and dark and black and white, and similarly opposing, irreconcilable forces. The word tension appears so many times that Wright had to cut out thirty instances of it in the final draft.

Among these oppositions the narrator becomes an immensely powerful but undefined force. Wright himself said, "One of the things that made me write is that I realize that I'm a very average Negro ... maybe that's what makes me extraordinary." This recognition of the self as typical is frequent in black autobiography, where beleaguering social forces chain the writer to his race. On the other hand, Wright also said, "I'm merely using a familiar literary form to unload many of the memories that have piled up in me, and now are coming out." These views are quite incompatible, since an average person would not have to unload memories, and their rendering as competing forces in *Black Boy* is one of its greatest sources of interest—and tension.

UNINTENDED HOPE

But in spite of *Black Boy*'s insistent refusal to resolve the oppositions upon which it rests, the final six pages nonetheless attempt to summarize the preceding experiences, to explain them, give them a defined significance. Wright asks, "From where in this southern darkness had I caught a sense of freedom?" And he proceeds to answer his question. He argues that books alone had kept him "alive in a negatively vital way," and especially books by "Dreiser, Masters, Mencken, Anderson, and Lewis" which:

> seemed defensively critical of the straitened American environment. These writers seemed to feel that America could be shaped nearer the hearts of those who lived in it. And it was out of these novels and stories and articles, out of the emotional impact of imaginative constructions of heroic or tragic deeds, that I felt touching my face a tinge of warmth from an unseen light; and in my leaving I was groping toward that invisible light, always trying to keep my face so set and turned that I would not lose the hope of its faint promise, using it as my justification for action.

These final words counteract the paradoxes of the epigraph. The black boy who was heading North was still blind at noonday, but he felt "warmth from an unseen light," and that warmth was hope. He was groping, but groping toward something. The ultimate paragraph states that Wright's search was for the essential significance of life. "With ever watchful eyes and bearing scars, visible and invisible, I headed North, full of a hazy notion that life could be lived with dignity, that the personalities of others should not be violated, that men should be able to confront other men without fear or shame, and that if men were lucky in their living on earth they might win some redeeming meaning for their having struggled and suffered here beneath the stars." Even though this last paragraph is presented conditionally, it is strong and eloquent. The promise, even the faint promise, of "redeeming meaning" seems adequate to the dignity of "having struggled and suffered here beneath the stars." We feel that hunger has at last changed to hope.

But this final statement, wrapping up and rounding out the book, is not what Wright had originally planned to publish when he finished *Black Boy* in December of 1943. As is now well known, the book was half again as long and its title was *American Hunger.* It reached page proofs and its jacket was designed. The full autobiography ends in 1937, ten years later than *Black Boy*, only six years before the actual writing of the book. Therefore, Wright had not achieved the sort of distance from his material which the shortened *Black Boy* implied. Partly for this reason, the full *American Hunger*—as distinct from the published *Black Boy*—retains that tentativeness which is the hallmark of the open autobiography.

In addition, the omitted second section of the autobiography expresses the tensions, the unresolved conflicts, of the first. *American Hunger* is the story, chiefly, of Wright's unsatisfying relationship with the Communist Party. Here, the themes of black and white are more subdued, but the theme of hunger persists and becomes more elaborate and universal. Of course, the question of black and white as a simple issue of race continues, but as Wright notes, he now feels "a different sort of tension," a different kind of "insecurity." The distinction now is likely to be animal and human, dirty and clean. A re-consideration of *Black Boy*'s epigraph will best illustrate the qualities of the omitted section and its relationship to the whole.

MEANING THROUGH EPIGRAPHS

The epigraph from Job which prefaced Black Boy was originally meant to summarize the entire *American Hunger.* The first line, "They meet with darkness in the daytime," as shown above summarizes the action of *Black Boy.* The second line, "And they grope at noonday as in the night, . . ." although not denying the content of *Black Boy*, more properly applies to the second section of the book. When Wright first enters a John Reed Club, it seems that neither he nor the members of the club need to grope; they ignore his blackness, and he feels for the first time totally human. But soon they begin to reduce his humanity in other ways. The Communists thwart his attempts to write biographies of their black members. "I had embraced their aims with the freest impulse I had ever known. I, the chary cynic, the man who had felt that no idea on earth was worthy of self-sacrifice, had publicly identified myself with them, and now their suspicion of me hit me with a terrific impact, froze me within. I groped in the noon sun." The isolation Wright feels is different from what he experienced in the South, but it is in some ways more terrible. He is still blind, groping even in the sunshine.

Wright had also picked separate epigraphs and titles for each of the subdivisions of the original *American Hunger*, and when these are properly replaced, they reassert the anxiety, hunger, and searching. In its original form, *Black Boy-American Hunger* had specific titles for each book, and each book carried a separate epigraph. *Black Boy* was to be called "Southern Night," and its epigraph was also from Job: "His strength shall be hunger-bitten, / And destruction shall be ready at his side." The dark imagery of the "Southern Night" fulfilled its title, as did its violence and hunger. The second part was to be called "The Horror and the Glory," and its epigraph came from a Negro Folk Song:

> Sometimes I wonder, huh,
> Wonder if other people wonder, huh,
> Sometimes I wonder, huh,
> Wonder if other people wonder, huh,
> Just like I do, oh my Lord, just like I do!

This brief verse indicates tentativeness, indecision, and a total lack of communication. In company with this resistance to conclusiveness, Wright emphasizes throughout his sense of wonder, his innocence: "how wide and innocent were my eyes, as round and open and dew-wet as morning-glories." Besides elaborating on its epigraph, the section called "The Horror and the Glory" explicitly defines its subtitle. In a climactic scene toward the end of the book, Wright's friend Ross confesses in an open trial that he has fought the policies of his fellow Communists. The glory of this moment is that Ross "had shared and accepted the vision that had crushed him," the vision that all men are equal and sharing in a communal world. But the horror is that this vision has been oversimplified by its followers, that they have allowed the Party to truncate their abilities to think. Wright says, "This, to me, was a spectacle of glory; and yet, because it had condemned me, because it was blind and ignorant, I felt that it was a spectacle of horror." Wright is a writer, and as such it is his business to search deep into the human heart, to name blindness when he sees it. This is of necessity a lonely search, and a complex one. . . .

The final pages of the full *American Hunger*, unlike those of the revised *Black Boy*, do not in fact explain how Wright managed to separate himself from his black confrères in the south how he became a writer. They do not even hint at his future successes, but rather at his sense of quest, and as Michel Fabre has put it, his feeling that the quest was unfinished and perhaps unfinishable. Wright did not plan to create in his readers nor to accept in himself a feeling of satisfaction, but of hunger, "a sense of the hunger for life that gnaws in us all." Here, too, Wright returns to his imagery of darkness and light: "Perhaps, I thought, out of my tortured feelings I could fling a spark into this darkness.". . . Wright knows that his effort is tentative and minimal, but also that he must try to write on the "white paper": "I would hurl words into this darkness and wait for an echo, and if an echo sounded, no matter how faintly, I would send other words to tell, to march, to fight, to create a sense of the hunger for life that gnaws in us all, to keep alive in our hearts a sense of the inexpressibly human." This statement is an admission that Wright cannot produce a work that is neat and conclusive, and as a result the content and effect of these final pages clash with the revised ending of *Black Boy*. . . .

CHANGES AND ADDITIONS

The search for truth, for as much truth as one can possibly set down, is the primary motive of a writer of an open as opposed to a defined autobiography. He is not trying primarily to please an audience, to create an aesthetically satisfying whole, but to look into his heart. . . .

When Wright had at last, through a multitude of drafts, faced and finished these truths and these terrors, he forwarded his manuscript to his agent, Paul Reynolds. Reynolds sent the manuscript, which was at that moment called "Black Hunger," to Harper's, where his editor Edward Aswell was expecting the novel about the problems of attempting to "pass." Aswell instantly recognized the autobiography's worth, however, and within three days had sent an advance. By this time the title was "American Hunger." The unsigned reader's notes (presumably Aswell's) preserved in the Harper papers suggest, among other things, that Wright cut out some of the John Reed section. The reader adds, "I may be wrong but I personally would like to see some of this cut and the story carried on to the years of Wright's success—

perhaps to the writing of *Native Son.* His own feeling of
hope, his own preservation through adversity would somehow be justified as it is not here." It is an editor's business to
ask that even lives be given justification, that order be imposed, that readers be given a sense of wholeness and com-
pletion. The suggestion that the autobiography be brought
up to *Native Son* was somehow dropped, but Wright cut the
John Reed section as much as he could. He rewrote the ending, but it resisted closure: "I tried and tried to strengthen
the ending. One thing is certain, I cannot step outside of the
mood rendered there and say anything without its sounding
false. So, what I've done is this: I've expanded the end to
deepen the mood, to hint at some kind of emotional resolution." The book moved toward its final stages. Wright objected to the phrase "courageous Negro" in the jacket copy
and asked that it be changed to "Negro American," which
"keeps the book related to the American scene and emphasizes the oneness of impulse, the singleness of aim of both
black and white Americans." Wright's emphasis, once again,
is on a general audience. He is trying to tell the truth, avoid-
ing the need to mask, modify, change, which had characterized his life in white America. He is deviating from the
model of the black slave narrative, which moved teleologi-
cally from slavery into freedom, from dehumanization to
fulfillment. The pressure to round out the book was strong,
but Wright successfully resisted.

The further metamorphosis, the addition of the final six
pages to *Black Boy,* took place in the Spring of 1944, after
American Hunger in its entirety had been forwarded to the
Book-of-the-Month Club. There, the judges said that they
would accept the book on condition that the second section
be cut off and the first section be provided with more complete resolution....

Dorothy Canfield Fisher, who had written the introduction
for *Native Son,* urged Wright to expand somewhat on his first
draft, and to seek out the American sources for his feelings of
hope.... Reflecting similar fervor, Aswell's list of possible titles for the truncated first half of *American Hunger* includes
besides fifteen evocations of darkness such as "Raw Hunger"
and "The Valley of Fear," these familiar complacencies: "Land
of the Free" and "Land of Liberty." Wright replied that the Negro environment was such that very few could intuit the
American way. Even these could desire nothing specific; they

could feel only a hope, a hunger. He emphasized that accident, not fate or choice, had more often than not governed his own life. However, Fisher had suggested that Wright consider which American books might have influenced him, given him a vision of America which had inspired him. In response to this request, Wright added two more paragraphs. One defined his hope—or more precisely refused to define his hope, showing that he was simply running away from violence and darkness, not toward anything he could formulate. The second paragraph had to do with his reading. Although Wright was careful to emphasize that his reading had been accidental, that the books were alien, that Theodore Dreiser, Edgar Lee Masters, H.L. Mencken, Sherwood Anderson, and Sinclair Lewis were critical of the American environment, he did give his hope a nearer reality. Even so, as mentioned above, he called it "a warmth from an unseen light," a phrase which Fisher praised with special emphasis. Wright had actually transported this phrase from *American Hunger*, where it appeared in a much more nebulous context: "Even so, I floundered, staggered; but somehow I always groped my way back to that path where I felt a tinge of warmth from an unseen light." Here there is blindness, the groping of the epigraph, and a tiny waft of hope. The *Black Boy* context, too, mentions groping, but the rhetoric is more assured, the feeling more triumphant.

A New Title and Uneasy Success

Indeed, Wright realized that *American Hunger* was no longer an appropriate title for this transformed autobiography. The Book-of-the-Month Club suggested "The First Chapter," which would have emphasized the initiation theme and implied a sequel, but this choice seemed jejune. Wright himself eventually suggested *Black Boy;* and his accompanying comment emphasizes the unity he had attained by truncating his book: "Now, this is not very original, but I think it covers the book. It is honest. Straight. And many people say it to themselves when they see a Negro and wonder how he lives. . . . *Black Boy* seems to me to be not only a title, but also a kind of heading of the whole general theme." His suggested subtitles, however, retained the sense of process. Nearly all of them contained the word "anxiety." Eventually, however, the subtitle too reflected the pose of completeness. *Black Boy* became "A Record of Childhood and Youth."

No one will ever know how the original *American Hunger* would have fared after publication, but *Black Boy* became an instant best-seller. In 1945 it ranked fourth among non-fiction sales. The content was new and shocking, but even so, many readers noted the hopeful ending. Responses ranged from outrage through misunderstanding and biased readings to unalleviated praise.... One typical review ended: "Soon after this discovery of the great world of books, we find our black boy born of the Mississippi plantation, now nineteen, packing up his bags for new worlds and horizons in the North. The rest of the story is well-known." Readers of *Black Boy*, no matter what their race or persuasion, often made the easy leap from the trip North to best-sellerdom and success.

But for Wright himself this leap was not easy, as readers of *American Hunger* know. Although pieces of the end of the original *American Hunger* were published in the *Atlantic Monthly* and *Mademoiselle* before *Black Boy* itself actually appeared, it obviously could not reach as large an audience as *Black Boy* itself. Constance Webb produced a photo-offset version of the whole manuscript, but this was only privately circulated. Even readers who later read most of this material in *The God that Failed* or in *Eight Men* could not intuit the negative strength of the omitted pages which immediately followed Wright's escape to the North in *American Hunger.* Nothing short of Wright's opening words can convey the desolation he felt on arriving in his hoped-for paradise: "My first glimpse of the flat black stretches of Chicago depressed and dismayed me, mocked all my fantasies." Wright did at last find a place where he was comfortable, but it was not Chicago or any other place in the United States. In spite of Mencken, Anderson, Dreiser, Masters, and Lewis, the American dream which Wright could not honestly elicit in the last pages of his *Black Boy* simply did not exist for him. When Wright arrived in Paris on 15 May 1946, he wrote to his editor at Harper's: "Ed, Paris is all I ever hoped to think it was, with a clear sky, buildings so beautiful with age that one wonders how they happen to be, and with people so assured and friendly and confident that one knows that it took many centuries of living to give them such poise. There is such an absence of race hate that it seems a little unreal. Above all, Paris strikes me as being truly a gentle city, with gentle manners." Here he could live and work as a human being, released from the ungentleness he could never escape in the United States.

A CALL FOR WRIGHT'S ORIGINAL MANUSCRIPT

In spite of the tentativeness of Wright's ending for *Black Boy*, in spite of his ultimate emigration, subsequent readers have continued to misread those final pages. Arthur P. Davis, for instance, in *From the Dark Tower* says, "The book ends . . . on a note of triumph. Near the close of the work Wright describes his moment of truth." But there was no moment of truth. Similarly, although Stephen Butterfield describes black autobiography in general as reflecting "a kind of cultural schizophrenia, where the author must somehow discover roots in a country which does not accept him as a human being," he defines *Black Boy* as one of the modern survivals of the pattern of the slave narrative. In support of this argument, he writes, "The slave narrative's basic pattern, it will be remembered, was an escape from South to North as well as a movement up the social scale from the status of slave to that of respected, educated citizen and vanguard of black politics and culture." Without the *American Hunger* ending, *Black Boy* is indeed modeled on the slave-narrative pattern, but Wright intended the ending to remain ambiguous, groping, hungry. Unfortunately the pattern absorbs the deviating elements, and only an unusually careful reader will notice the hesitancy in the final pages, the conditional verbs, the haltered rhetoric, the mention of luck.

In 1977, seventeen years after Wright's death, Harper and Row published *American Hunger* as a separate volume, with an afterword by Michel Fabre giving a brief outline of its publishing history. Fabre objected to the disjoining of the two parts of the original autobiography, observing, "*Black Boy* is commonly construed as a typical success story, and thus it has been used by the American liberal to justify his own optimism regarding his country.". . .

Many books, through the influence of an editor, have been drastically changed before publication, and the published work is accepted as definitive. . . . It is true that Wright concurred entirely in the division of *American Hunger* into *Black Boy* and its sequel, even supplying the new title. But, as I have tried to show here, the change was more drastic than Wright meant it to be; the ultimate significance of the book shifted further than Wright had intended. *Black Boy* became a more definitive statement than its themes of hope and hunger could support. Therefore, *American Hunger* needs to be reissued in its entirety, with the final six pages of the present *Black Boy* given as an appendix. Failing this, every reader of *Black Boy* should buy both books and read them together, recognizing that the last six pages of *Black Boy* were added in a final revision in part as a response to wartime patriotism. When combined, both of these books emphasize the lack of conviction, the isolation, and finally the lack of order in Wright's world as he saw it, a sadness and disarray which his truncated autobiography *Black Boy*, as published, seems at the end to deny.

Black Boy as Art

Charles T. Davis

Wright scholar Charles T. Davis contends that artisti-
cally *Black Boy* is one of Wright's most successful
works, neither fact nor fiction as Wright skillfully
chooses which facts and incidents of his life to omit
from his story for the sake of theme or other creative
concerns. Some omissions include names of family
members and friends, some positive experiences
with whites, and any mention of male role models.
Wright's creative use of three narrative voices is another stylistic quality that helps define the book not
only as a story of a life, but as art.

Some critics, carried off by the impact of *Black Boy*, tend to
treat the autobiography as if it were fiction. They are influenced by the fact that much great modern fiction, James
Joyce's *Portrait of the Artist as a Young Man*, for example, is
very close to life. And the tendency here is reinforced by the
fact that the author himself, Wright, is a creator of fictions.
Yielding so is a mistake because many of the incidents in *Black
Boy* retain the sharp angularity of life, rather than fitting into
the dramatic or symbolic patterns of fiction. Richard's setting
fire to the "fluffy white curtains," and incidentally the house,
is not the announcement of the birth of a pyromaniac or a rev-
olutionary, but testimony primarily to the ingenuity of a small
black boy in overcoming mundane tedium. We must say "primarily" because this irresponsible act suggests the profound
distress and confusion an older Richard would bring to a family that relied heavily upon rigid attitudes toward religion, expected behavior, and an appropriate adjustment to Southern
life. . . . Nor does Richard's immodest invitation to his grandmother during his bath offer disturbing witness of the emergence of a pornographer or a connoisseur of the erotic; rather,
it points to something more general, the singular perversity in

Richard that makes him resist family and the South. In *Black Boy* we exist in a world of limited probability that is not life exactly, because there is an order to be demonstrated, and it does not display the perfect design of a serious fiction. We occupy a gray area in between. The patterns are here on several levels. Though they may not be so clear and tight as to permit the critic to predict, they do govern the selection of materials, the rendering of special emphases, distortions, and the style.

WHY THE OMISSION? THERE ARE NO NAMES OR FRIENDS IN THE TEXT

We seldom raise questions about what is omitted from an autobiography, yet if we wish to discover pattern, we must begin with what we do not find. . . . *Black Boy* profits from rigorous and inspired editing. One function of the omissions is to strengthen the impression in our minds of Richard's intense isolation. This is no mean achievement given the fact that Wright was born into a large family (on his mother's side, at least) which, despite differences in personality, cooperated in times of need. The father, because of his desertion of his mother, was early in Richard's mind, perhaps in the sentiments of other family members, too, an object of hate and scorn. There are no names in the early pages of *Black Boy*, not even that of Richard's brother, Leon Allan, just a little more than two years younger than Richard. When the names begin to appear in *Black Boy*, they tend to define the objects of adversary, often violently hostile relationships—Grandmother Wilson, Aunt Addie, Uncle Thomas. Two notable exceptions are Grandfather Wilson, an ineffectual man capable only of reliving his past as a soldier in the Civil War, and Richard's mother, Ella, a pathetically vulnerable woman of some original strength who, because of continuing illness, slipped gradually into a state of helplessness that became for Richard symbolic of his whole life as a black boy in the South.

The admirable biography of Wright by Michel Fabre suggests another dimension for Richard's opponents in his embattled household. The climax of the violence in the family occurred with the confrontation with Uncle Tom, portrayed as a retired and defeated schoolteacher reduced at the time to earning a living by performing odd jobs as a carpenter. Richard resented the fact that he was the victim of Uncle

Tom's frustrations, and he responded to orders from the older man by threatening him with razors in both hands and by spitting out hysterically, "You are not an example to me; you could never be. . . . You're a *warning*. Your life isn't so hot that you can tell me what to do. . . . Do you think that I want to grow up and weave the bottoms of chairs for people to sit in?" A footnote from Fabre adds more information about the humiliated uncle:

> The portrait of Uncle Thomas in *Black Boy* is exaggerated. After living with the Wilsons, he moved next door and became a real-estate broker. In 1938, he was a member of the Executive Committee of the Citizen's Civic League in Jackson and wrote a book on the word *Negro*, discussing the superiority complex of the Whites and its effects on the Blacks. At this time Richard put him in contact with Doubleday publishers and the uncle and the nephew were completely reconciled.

. . . But *Black Boy* contains no softening reconsiderations of Uncle Tom, or of Aunt Addie, who, like her brother, seems to have possessed some redeeming qualities, or of Granny Wilson for that matter. Their stark portraits dominate the family and define a living space too narrow, too mean, and too filled with frustration and poverty for an imaginative youngster like Richard.

A growing boy, when denied the satisfactions of a loving home, looks for emotional support at school or at play, and if he is lucky, he finds something that moderates domestic discontent. But there is little compensation of this sort in *Black Boy*. The reality of the life away from the family seems to be less bleak than Wright represents it, though his schooling was retarded by early irregularity because of the family's frequent moves, and his play restricted, perhaps, because of the family's desperate need for money and Granny's Seventh Day Adventist scruples. Once again we are struck by the absence of names—of teachers like Lucy McCranie and Alice Burnett, who taught Richard at the Jim Hill School in Jackson and recognized his lively intelligence, or Mary L. Morrison or the Reverend Otto B. Cobbins, Richard's instructors in the eighth and ninth grades of the Smith-Robinson School, to whose dedication and competence, despite personal limitations, Wright paid tribute elsewhere. There was no question about his marginal status in these institutions, since Richard stood regularly at the head of his class.

Black Boy is singularly devoid of references to rewarding peer associations. There is no mention of Dick Jordan, Joe

Brown, Perry Booker, or Essie Lee Ward, friends of this period and so valued that Wright was in touch with several of
them ten years later when he was living in Chicago. The fact
that a few of Wright's childhood associates did succeed in
making their way to Chicago has an amount of interest in itself, serving, as well, to break the isolation that Wright has
fabricated so well. Among the childhood activities that went
unrecorded were the exploits of the Dick Wright clan, made
up of a group of neighborhood boys who honored in the
name of their society, no doubt, their most imaginative
member. The clan included Dick Jordan, Perry Booker, Joe
Brown, and also Frank Sims, a descendant of a black sena-
tor during the Reconstruction period, Blanche K. Bruce.
What is amply clear, then, is that Wright had a childhood
more than a little touched by the usual rituals and preoccupations of middle-class boys growing up in America, but
what is also apparent is that reference to them would modify our sense of Richard's deprived and disturbed emotional
life, a necessity for the art of the autobiography, rather more
important than any concern for absolute accuracy.

THE OMISSION OF SEX AND MALE ROLE MODELS

Wright has little to say directly about sex. Richard's most serious temptation for sexual adventure comes toward the end
of *Black Boy* in Memphis, when he is taken in by the Moss
family. Richard succeeds in resisting the opportunity to take
advantage of a cozy arrangement with Bess, the daughter
whom Mrs. Moss seeks to thrust upon him, with marriage as
her ultimate objective. There are some indirect references to
frustrated, sublimated, or distorted forms of sexual energy–
–in Miss Simon, certainly, the tall, gaunt, mulatto woman
who ran the orphan home where Richard was deposited for
a period. And there were exposures to white women, all calculated to teach Richard the strength of the taboo prohibit-
ing the thought (not to mention the fact) of black-white sexual relations in the South. But Richard never takes an
aggressive interest in sex; the adventures that he stumbles
into create traumas when they are serious and unavoidable,
or are embarrassing when he can resist participation and
control his reactions. . . . It is strange that so little space is
given to sexual episodes and fantasies in the record of the
gradual maturing of an adolescent—unbelievable, given the
preoccupations of the twentieth century. We face the prob-

lem of omission again. Wright deliberately seeks to deprive his hero, his younger self, of any substantial basis for sensual gratification located outside his developing imagination. The world that *Black Boy* presents is uniformly bleak, always ascetic, and potentially violent, and the posture of the isolated hero, cut off from family, peer, or community support, is rigidly defiant, without the softening effects of interludes of sexual indulgence.

Richard's immediate world, not that foreign country controlled by whites, is overwhelmingly feminine. Male contacts are gone, except for occasional encounters with uncles. The father has deserted his home, and the grandfather is lost in the memories of "The War." The uncles tend to make brief entrances and exits, following the pattern of Hoskins, quickly killed off by envious whites in Arkansas, or the unnamed new uncle, forced to flee because of unstated crimes against whites. Thomas is the uncle who stays around somewhat longer than the others do, long enough to serve as the convenient object for Richard's mounting rebellion. The encounter with Uncle Tom is the culminating episode marking a defiance expressed earlier against a number of authority figures, all women—Richard's mother, Miss Simon, Grandmother Wilson, Aunt Addie. Women dominate in Richard's world, with the ultimate authority vested in Granny—nearwhite, uncompromising, unloving, and fanatical, daring Richard to desecrate her Seventh Day Adventist Sabbath. The only relief from feminine piety is the pathetic schoolteacher who, in a happy moment, tells an enraptured Richard about Bluebeard and his wives. But even this delight, moved in part, no doubt, by Bluebeard's relentless war against females, is short-lived. Granny puts a stop to such sinning, not recognizing, of course, the working out of the law of compensation.

SURVIVAL: WRIGHT DOESN'T TELL IT ALL

Richard's odyssey takes him from the black world to the white—from the problems of home and family to new and even more formidable difficulties. The movement is outward into the world, to confront an environment that is not controlled by Granny, though it provides much that contributes to an explanation of Granny's behavior. Richard's life among blacks emphasizes two kinds of struggle. One is simply the battle for physical existence, the need for food, clothing, shelter, and protection that is the overwhelming concern of the early pages of *Black Boy*. The second grows out of Richard's deeply felt desire to acquire his own male identity, a sense of self apart from a family that exerts increasing pressure upon this growing black boy to behave properly, to experience Christian conversion, and to accept guidance from his (mostly female) elders. Survival in two senses, then, is the dominant theme, one which does not change when he leaves the black community. The terms are the same though the landscape is new. Richard desperately seeks employment in white neighborhoods and in the downtown business districts in order to contribute to the support of his family. He discovers, when he does so, that the demand to accommodate becomes even more insistent and less flexible than that exerted by his own family.

The difference is that the stakes are higher. Richard thinks he must find a job, any job, to earn a living. This awareness represents a step beyond the simple dependence that moves a small boy to complain, "Mama, I'm hungry." If he does not find work, Richard feels that he has failed his family in an essential way and made its survival precarious. Though his independence in the black world leads to harsh sanctions—threats, bed without supper, whippings—he is not prepared for the infinitely greater severity of the white world. It is cruel, calculating, and sadistic. Richard never doubts that he will survive the lashings received from his mother, Granny, and assorted aunts and uncles, but he does question his ability to endure exposure to whites. The ways of white folks are capricious and almost uniformly malignant. Richard understands that the penalty for non-conformity, down to the way a black boy walks or holds his head, is not simply a sore body, but death. When Richard gives up a good job with an optical company, with a chance, according to his boss, to become something more than a menial worker, he does so because of the opposition exhibited by whites who think he aspires to do "*white* man's work." Richard confides to his boss when he leaves the factory: "I'm scared. . . . They would kill me."

From the woman who inquires of Richard, looking for yet another job, "Boy, do you steal?" to the two young men who attempt to arrange for Richard to fight another black boy for the amusement of an assembly of whites, we witness an unrelieved set of abuses. Certainly omission of some mitigating circumstances and artful distortion are involved in this bitter report. Richard is gradually introduced to a white world that grows progressively more dominant, divisive, and corrupting concerning the black life that serves it. Richard understands fully what is expected of him:

> I began to marvel at how smoothly the black boys acted out the roles that the white race had mapped out for them. Most of them were not conscious of living a special, separate, stunted way of life. Yet I know that in some period of their growing up—a period that they had no doubt forgotten—there had been developed in them a delicate, sensitive controlling mechanism that shut off their minds and emotions from all that the white race had said was taboo.

In Wright's South it was unthinkable for a black boy to aspire to become a lens-grinder, much less to harbor the ambition to become a writer. When Richard is thoughtless enough to reveal his true aim in life to one of his white employers, the response is predictable: "You'll never be a writer.... Who on earth put such ideas into your nigger head?" Given his difficulties in adjusting to an oppressive Southern system, Richard sustains his interest in writing through a monumental act of will. We are led to the inevitable conclusion that Richard must flee the South if he is to remain alive, and the desire to achieve an artistic career seems less important in light of the more basic concern for life itself.

We have every reason to suspect that the treatment of whites gains a certain strength from artistic deletion, too. Michel Fabre points out that Wright's relationship with a white family named Wall does not fit the pattern of abuse and brutal exploitation that emerges from the autobiography: "Although *Black Boy* was designed to describe the effects of racism on a black child, which meant omitting incidents tending to exonerate white persons in any way, there is no doubt that the Walls were liberal and generous employers. For almost two years Richard worked before and after class, earning three dollars a week bringing in firewood and doing the heavy cleaning." Fabre adds, with reference especially to Mrs. Wall and her mother, "Since they respected his qualities as an individual, he sometimes submitted his problems and plans to them and soon considered their house a second home where he met with more understanding than from his own family." This is not matter that reinforces a design displaying increasing difficulty for Richard as he moves outward and into contact with white society. Nor does it support Richard's growing conviction that his survival depends upon his escape from the South. The design of *Black Boy* offers an accelerating pattern of confrontations, taking into account both an increase in danger for Richard and a mounting seriousness in terms of society's estimate of his deviations. Like Big Boy, Richard must flee or die.

WRIGHT'S THREE NARRATIVE VOICES

The narrator of *Black Boy* has three voices. The simplest records recollected events with clarity and a show of objectivity. We may be troubled by an insufficient context surrounding or an inadequate connection linking these episodes until we become aware of the suggestion of a psychological dimension for them. The incidents illustrate basic emotions: the discovery of fear and guilt, first, when fire destroys Richard's house; the experience of hate, directed this time toward the father, in killing the kitten; the satisfactions of violence, in defeating the teenage gang; the dangers of curiosity about the adult world, in Richard's early addiction to alcohol. The psyche of a child takes shape through exposure to a set of unusual traumas, and the child goes forth, as we have seen, into a world that becomes progressively more brutal and violent. Style in this way reinforces the first theme of the autobiography, survival.

It is in hearing the more complicated and lyrical second voice of the narrator that we sense for the first time another theme in the autobiography. This is the making of the artist. The world, we have been told, is cold, harsh, and cruel, a fact which makes all the more miraculous the emergence of a literary imagination destined to confront it. The bleak South, by some strange necessity, is forced to permit the blooming of a single rose. Wright expends upon the nourishment of this tender plant the care that he has given to describing the sterile soil from which it springs.

A third, didactic voice offers occasional explanations of the matter recorded by the other two. It comments at times upon the lack of love among blacks in the South, the distortions in human relationships involving blacks and whites, and corruption in the social and economic systems. At other times it advises us of the necessity for secrecy when a black boy harbors the ambition to write, and explains the difficulties which he confronts when he seeks to serve an apprenticeship to his art. Despite formidable opposition and the danger of complete isolation, this ambition lives and forces the growth of Richard's imaginative powers.

We do not begin simply with the statement of the intention to become an artist. We start, rather, . . . with the sense experience that rests behind the word. Richard's memory offers rich testimony of the capacity to feel objects of nature, small and large. Not only these. We note that accompanying the record of sensations is the tendency to translate sensation into an appropriate emotion—melancholy, nostalgia, astonishment, disdain. All of the senses achieve recognition in Richard's memory, and all combine to emphasize memories of violent experiences: the killing of the chicken; the shocking movement of the snake; the awesome golden glow on a silent night.

DETACHMENT, IMAGINATION, AND USE OF SYMBOLS

Apart from this basic repository of sensation and image, we sense early in Richard two other qualities just as essential to the budding artist. One is detachment, the feeling of being different from others. In two worlds to which he is exposed, that of the family and then the more muddled arena of affairs, he rejects all efforts to moderate his apartness. Though conversion and subsequent baptism apparently point to joining the company of the saved, viewed in the conventional way, damnation is assured by the refusal to deliver the right kind of valedictory at the graduation exercises of his grammar school. Barely passing one ritual, he flunks another. He maintains under pressure his status as an alien, so ultimately he will be free to exercise the imagination that faces the cold world.

The second quality is curiosity. His mother tells Richard that he asks too many questions. Our young hero is apparently undaunted by the fact that his insistent prying has led to one of the earliest addictions to alcohol recorded in literature. But another addiction is more serious, to the truth in the appearances about him. "Will you stop asking silly questions!" his mother commands. About names, about color, about the relationship between the two. Curiosity constantly leads Richard to forbidden areas more menacing than the saloon, to the mysterious privileged province of whites in Mississippi and the equally mysterious restriction of the blacks.

A neat form of inversion is involved in the development of Richard's artistic talent. We note that the qualities supporting and sustaining the growing boy's imagination are just those preventing a successful adjustment to life in the South. To achieve a tolerable existence, not even a comfortable one, Richard must have firm relationships with the members of his family and with his neighbors and peers; to survive in the larger, white-dominated society he must accept without questioning the inflexible system of Southern mores and customs. Richard, rejecting these imperatives, responds to the demands of his own imagination.

Richard's sensations in nature anticipate a discovery just as valuable and far reaching. This is literature itself. Of the encounter with *Bluebeard* Richard says, "My sense of life deepened. . . ." He recalls, further, a total emotional response, emphasized, no doubt, by the background of an unresponding family, and he realizes that he stands on the threshold of a "gateway to a forbidden and enchanting land." So, early, the opposition is clear. On the one hand is the bleak environment frowning upon any activity of the imagination, whether passive or active, and on the other a determined Richard who will not be turned aside. His reading would be done in secret, a clandestine activity abetted by delivering racist newspapers and borrowing the library card of a compliant white man. There is no evidence that he discussed his reading with anyone, black or white. . . .

Richard's commitment to write precipitates confrontations. As we have seen, his honest admission of this aspiration to one white lady employer results in bitter ridicule, and Richard feels, despite the pressures of his situation, that his ego has been assaulted. His first publication, "The Voodoo of Hell's Half-Acre," is little more than the crude rendering of the stuff of *Flynn's Detective Weekly*, but Richard discovers that printing it is an act of defiance, further separating him from the world that surrounds him, both black and white.

Richard does not intend to restrict his range to any half-acre, though his first is identified as "Hell." His province would be the real world around him. True, it is sometimes not to be distinguished from the subject area defined by his first literary effort. At a very young age Richard sees "elephants" moving across the land—not real "elephants," but convicts in a chain gang, and the child's awe is prompted by the unfortunate confusion of elephant and zebra. An inauspicious beginning, perhaps, but the pattern of applying his imagination to his immediate surrounding is firmly set. Later, Richard says more soberly that he rejects religion because it ignores immediate reality. His faith, predictably, must be wedded to "common realities of life," anchored in the sensations of his body and in what his mind could grasp. This is, we see, an excellent credo for an artist, but a worthless one for a black boy growing to maturity in Mississippi.

Another piece of evidence announcing Richard's talent is the compulsion to make symbols of the details of his everyday experience. This faculty is early demonstrated in his tendency to generalize from sensational experience, to define an appropriate emotion to associate with his feelings. A more highly developed example is Richard's reaction to his mother's illness and sufferings, representative for him in later years of the poverty, the ignorance, the helplessness of black life in Mississippi. And it is based on the generalizing process that Richard is a black boy, any black boy experiencing childhood, adolescence, and early manhood in the South.

Richard leaves the South. He must, to survive as a man and to develop as an artist. By the time we reach the end of the narrative, these two drives have merged. We know, as well, that the South will never leave Richard, never depart from the rich imagination that developed despite monumental opposition. We have only the final promise that Richard will someday understand the region that has indelibly marked him.

Richard's ultimate liberation, and his ultimate triumph, will be the ability to face the dreadful experience in the South and to record it. . . . But he has left us at the conclusion of *Black Boy*, with a feeling that is less than happy. He has yet to become an artist. Then we realize with a start what we have read is not simply the statement of a promise, its background and its development, but its fulfillment. Wright has succeeded in reconstructing the reality that was for a long time perhaps too painful to order, and that reconstruction may be Wright's supreme artistic achievement, *Black Boy*.

Lies in *Black Boy*

Timothy Dow Adams

An assistant professor of English at West Virginia University, Timothy Dow Adams suggests that Wright's autobiography is full of half-truths, omissions, and blatant lies because the circumstances of his youth prevented him from hearing or speaking truths. Lying, Adams says, becomes a metaphor for the self in *Black Boy* that is complicated by Wright's three audiences: actual, authorial, and narrative.

Since the publication of *Black Boy* in 1945, reactions to its authenticity have been curiously contradictory, often mutually exclusive. For many readers the book is particularly honest, sincere, open, convincing and accurate. But for others *Black Boy* leaves a feeling of inauthenticity, a sense that the story or its author is not to be trusted. These conflicting reactions are best illustrated by the following representative observations by Ralph White and W.E.B. Du Bois. White, a psychologist, identified "ruthless honesty" as "the outstanding quality which made the book not only moving but also intellectually satisfying." But Du Bois noted that while "nothing that Richard Wright says is in itself unbelievable or impossible; it is the total picture that is not convincing." Attempting to reconcile these opposing views, I wish to argue that both sides are correct, that the book is one of the most truthful accounts of the black experience in America, even though the protagonist's story often does not ring true, and that this inability to tell the truth is Wright's major metaphor of self. A repeated pattern of misrepresentation becomes the author's way of making us believe that his personality, his family, his race—his whole childhood and youth—conspired to prevent him from hearing the truth, speaking the truth, or even being believed unless he lied.

In terms of truth, we expect from an autobiography obedience to the conventions of the genre which hold that the

Excerpted from Timothy Dow Adams, "I Do Believe Him Though I Know He Lies: Lying as Genre and Metaphor in *Black Boy*," *Prose Studies*, vol. 8, no. 2 (September 1985). Copyright Frank Cass & Co. Ltd. Reprinted by permission of the publisher, Frank Cass & Company, 900 Eastern Ave., Ilford, Essex, England.

story being presented is a significant part of a person's life, written in retrospect by the subject of the story, who purports to believe that he or she is telling a truthful version of the past. The reader expects, even enjoys, detecting misrepresentations, odd emphasis, telling omissions, and over and under determination, and will willingly overlook factual errors, but for most readers an autobiography is dishonest if the author does not seem to be trying to tell the overall truth. I agree with A.O.J. Cockshut's assertion that "the simple truth of accurate record of facts is clearly important; but as a rule this is overshadowed by other kinds. . . .

For most contemporary readers worries about *Black Boy's* trustworthiness stemmed from questions of genre: although the book was clearly not called "The Autobiography of Richard Wright," its subtitle—"A Record of Childhood and Youth"—did suggest autobiography. The following descriptions of *Black Boy* reflect the confusion of readers: biography, autobiographical story, fictionalized biography, a masterpiece of romanced facts, a sort-of-autobiography, pseudo-autobiography, part fiction/part truth, autobiography with the quality of fiction, and case history.

Some of these generic confusions were generated by Wright's statements about his creation; he meant the work to be collective autobiography, a personalized record of countless black Americans growing up with a personal history of hunger, deprivation, and constant racism. He also remarked that he decided to write his life story after giving an autobiographical talk to a racially mixed audience at Fisk University in Nashville in 1943. . . . Using truthfulness as his watchword, Wright began *Black Boy* as an attempt to set the record straight, including his personal one, which already consisted of a number of "biographies of the author" or "notes on contributors" written by himself in the third person, sometimes with exaggerated accounts of his youth. . . .

Most revelatory about the conflict between his intentions and the actual writing of his personal narrative is the following observation from a newspaper article called "The Birth of Black Boy":

> The real hard terror of writing like this came when I found
> that writing of one's life was vastly different from speaking of
> it. I was rendering a close and emotionally connected ac-
> count of my experience and the ease I had had in speaking
> from notes at Fisk would not come again. I found that to tell

> the truth is the hardest thing on earth, harder than fighting in a war, harder than taking part in a revolution. If you try it, you will find that at times sweat will break upon you. You will find that even if you succeed in discounting the attitudes of others to you and your life, you must wrestle with yourself most of all, fight with yourself; for there will surge up in you a strong desire to alter facts, to dress up your feelings. You'll find that there are many things that you don't want to admit about yourself and others. As your record shapes itself an awed wonder haunts you. And yet there is no more exciting an adventure than trying to be honest in this way. The clean, strong feeling that sweeps you when you've done it makes you know that.

Although Wright seemed unsure of his book's generic identity, he never referred to *Black Boy* as an autobiography. . . . Constance Webb reports that Wright was uneasy with the word *autobiography*, both because of "an inner distaste for revealing in first person instead of through a fictitious character the dread and fear and anguished self-questioning of his life" and because he realized he would write his story using "portions of his own childhood, stories told him by friends, things he had observed happening to others" and fictional techniques.

Although some readers see Wright as unsuccessful in his struggle neither "to alter facts" nor to "dress up feelings," the book's tendency to intermix fiction and fact is clearly part of both Wright's personal literary history and the Afro-American literary tradition in which he was writing. The form of *Black Boy* partly imitates the traditional slave narrative, a literary type which allowed for a high degree of fictionality in the cause of abolition. . . .

Richard Wright makes clear that *Black Boy* is not meant as a traditional autobiography by presenting much of the story in the form of dialogue marked with quotation marks, which suggests the unusual degree of fiction within his factual story. . . . Writing *Black Boy* in the spirit of folk history seemed a reasonable thing to do, and Wright apparently saw no hypocrisy in omitting personal details which did not contribute to what he was simultaneously thinking of as his own story and the story of millions of others. Wright's claim to be composing the autobiography of a generic black child is reinforced by the narrator's particular reaction to racism: "The things that influenced my conduct as a Negro did not have to happen to me directly; I needed but to hear of them to feel their full effects in the deepest layers of my consciousness."

OMISSIONS AND BLATANT LIES

Roy Pascal is correct in asserting that "where a lie is the result of a calculated intention to appear right or important, danger is done to autobiographical truth" and that "the most frequent cause of failure in autobiography is an untruthfulness which arises from the desire to appear admirable." However, most of the omission in *Black Boy* is designed not to make the persona appear admirable, but to make Richard Wright into "black boy," to underplay his own family's middle-class ways and more positive values. He does not mention that his mother was a successful school teacher and that many of his friends were children of college faculty members; he omits most of his father's family background, and his own sexual experiences. Reactions from sensitive Southern whites are mainly left out, including those of the Wall family to whom, we learn from Michel Fabre's biography, "he sometimes submitted his problems and plans . . . and soon considered their house a second home where he met with more understanding than from his own family."

In addition to omissions, name changes, poetic interludes, and extensive dialogue, *Black Boy* is replete with questionable events that biographical research has revealed to be exaggerated, inaccurate, mistaken, or invented. . . . While these distortions are acceptable to many, especially in light of Wright's intention of using his life to show the effects of racism, there are numerous other manipulations less acceptable because more self-serving.

Most of these incidents are relatively minor, and so doubts seem unimportant; however, the misrepresentations in two of the book's most important episodes—the high school graduation speech and the story of Uncle Hoskins and the Mississippi River—might be less acceptable. "Black boy's" refusal to deliver the principal's graduation speech rather than his own is apparently based on truth, but the version in *Black Boy* leaves out the important fact that Wright rewrote his speech, cutting out more volatile passages as a compromise. The story of Uncle Hoskins does not ring true, for how could a boy whose life had been to that point so violent, be scared of his uncle's relatively harmless trick? One reason the tale feels false is that the story, complete with revelations about Uncle Hoskins such as "I never trusted him after that. Whenever I saw his face the memory of my terror upon the river would come back, vivid and strong, and it stood as a barrier between us," actually happened to Ralph Ellison who told it to Wright.

For many critics, including Edward Margolies, these deliberate manipulations reduce *Black Boy*'s authenticity as autobiography because they set up doubts about everything, the same doubts that resonate through the remarks of black writers from Du Bois to Baldwin to David Bradley, all of whom have persisted in taking *Black Boy*'s protagonist to be Richard Wright. But "Richard Wright is not the same person as the hero of that book, not the same as 'I' or 'Richard' or the 'Black boy,' not by several light years," argues James Olney, who refers to the book's chief character as "black boy," explaining that "'by means of an encompassing and creative memory, Richard Wright imagines it all, and he is as much the creator of the figure that he calls 'Richard' as he is of the figure that, in *Native Son*, he calls 'Bigger.'" Olney's idea that the central figure be treated as a single person referred to as "black boy," a literary character representing both the actual author as a child and the adult author—the famous writer imagining himself as representative of inarticulate black children—is finally convincing. That seems to be what Richard Wright meant to do, said he had done, and what he did. . . .

TRUTH IS IN THE EYE OF THE AUDIENCE

Part of the complication about lying in *Black Boy*—who is lying and to whom—derives from the interplay between audiences, the resonances between the actual audience, the authorial audience, and the narrative audience, to use Peter Rabinowitz's terms. The actual audience is the group of real humans holding *Black Boy* in their hands as they read. The authorial audience is the group Wright imagined himself addressing. The narrative audience, which Gerald Prince calls the narratee (*narrataire*), is the group of people to whom the narrator is speaking. Sorting out these audiences is particularly confusing but interesting in *Black Boy* because the book is autobiographical and therefore the relation between author and narrator is more complicated than in much fiction, and because both author and narrator are black. The important questions about the race, sex, and assumptions of the reader in the text are difficult to answer absolutely, but it seems clear that Richard Wright relates to the authorial audience as "black boy" does to the narrative audience. Because Wright's actual audience at Fisk University was racially mixed, and because he cited his speaking there as the specific impetus for writing the book, it is logical to assume that the authorial audience is composed of both black and white members. Because the book is dedicated to "ELLEN and JULIA," Wright's white wife and interracial daughter, it seems reasonable to assume that he thought of his authorial audience as being both male and female, black girls as well as black boys.

The question of the narrative audience is more complex, but I believe that the readers inscribed in and by the text, the audience to whom "black boy" is speaking, is also racially mixed. This audience is in one sense made up of all of the people described in the book, black and white, who failed to understand the narrator during his lifetime. At other times the narrator is addressing himself only to a white audience. . . . Although the authorial audience includes males and females, the narrative audience seems limited to males, as the narrator makes plain in such statements as "It was degrading to play with girls and in our talk we relegated them to a remote island of life."

These distinctions between audiences are important because the actual reader's attempt to react to the book properly, that is in the right spirit, is somewhat like the narrator's attempts to react properly to the different values in the black and white worlds. Lying to white people is one thing, lying to blacks another. And, as Wright discovered after his speech in Nashville, telling the truth to a mixed audience is more dangerous than separating the truth into white and black versions. When *Black Boy's* authorial and narrative audiences converge, the reader is the least likely to question the authenticity of the story. As the two audiences move apart, the reader begins to feel uneasy, partly because of trying to decide which audience to join. . . .

When confronted with *Black Boy's* deviations from absolute biographical truth, less sophisticated readers, such as students, are seldom bothered. They sense that discrepancies uncovered by reading other texts have little bearing on the truth of the text at hand. Nevertheless, the same students often respond unfavourably to what they perceive as inauthenticity arising from within *Black Boy*. . . . They experience what Barrett Mandel calls "dis-ease with the autobiography. It seems as if the author is lying (not, please, writing fiction), although readers cannot always easily put their finger on the lie."

The lying they sense centres on these three concerns: "black boy" is never wrong, is falsely naive, and is melodramatic, three characteristics of what Mandel refers to as autobiography in which "the ratification is negative—the light of now shines on the illusion the ego puts forth and reveals it as false." Mandel believes that most autobiographers are basically honest, but those who are not give themselves away through tone: "Since the ego is in conflict with the truth, the reader very often gets that message. The author has created an illusion of an illusion. . . . The tone is forever slipping away from the content, giving itself away." While Mandel does not include *Black Boy* in the category of dishonest autobiographies, instead citing it as a typical reworking of the past, many critics have echoed my students' concerns. For example, Robert Stepto finds fault with two early incidents in which "black boy" insists on the literal meaning of words: when he pretends to believe his father's injunction to kill a noisy kitten, and when he refuses ninety-seven cents for his dog because he wants a dollar. "The fact remains that *Black Boy* requires its readers to admire Wright's persona's remarkable and unassailable innocence in certain major episodes, and to condone his exploitation of that innocence in others," writes Stepto. "This, I think, is a poorly tailored seam, if not precisely a flaw, in *Black Boy's* narrative strategy." Rather than seeing these episodes, and others like them, as examples of bad faith or as rough edges in the narrative fabric, I see them as deliberate renderings of the terrible dilemma of black boys, and their need to dissemble about everything, especially about the nature of their naiveté. Wright's persona is confessing, not boasting. His family life and his difficulty with hypocrisy made lying at once a constant requirement for survival, and a nearly impossible performance, especially for a poor liar whose tone gives him away.

The inability to lie properly, exhibited in countless scenes, is "black boy's" major problem in adjusting to black/white relations in his youth. Asked by a potential white employer if he steals, "black boy" is incredulous: "Lady, if I was a thief, I'd never tell anybody," he replies. *Black Boy* is filled with episodes in which its hero is unable to lie, forced to lie, caught between conflicting lies, not believed unless he lies. Poorly constructed lies are appropriate metaphors to portray a boy whose efforts to set the record straight are as frustrated as his grandfather's attempts to claim a Navy pension, which is thwarted by bureaucratic error for his whole life. Falsehoods are an apt metaphor for the speech of a boy who distrusts everyone, himself included. . . .

WRIGHT PRESENTS THE EMOTIONAL TRUTH

In the novel's opening scenes Richard Wright has borrowed the rhetoric of the oral historian in consciously fictionalizing the story of the burning house and his subsequent punishment, while sending the reader signals that he has done so. He wants the reader to feel that there is something not quite right about the whole scene. That the three-year old brother can see the folly of playing with fire when the four-year old "black boy" cannot, that the reasons for setting the fire are as spurious as the explanation—"I had just wanted to see how the curtains would look when they burned" that the nightmarish description of white bags filled with foul liquid are obviously meant to be symbolic, and finally that the boy is chastened, not by his actions, but by the thought that his mother had come close to killing him—all these signals are meant to paint a truthful picture of a boy who later came to hold "a conviction that the meaning of living came only when one was struggling to wring a meaning out of meaningless suffering." The opening scene suggests the whole atmosphere of the book, a desperate fear of meaningless visitations of violence without context, a life of deliberate misrepresentations of the truth and complete distrust of all people, a world in which "each event spoke with a cryptic tongue." Throughout *Black Boy* Wright presents a lonely figure whose life does not ring true because "that's the way things were between whites and blacks in the South; many of the most important things were never openly said; they were understated and left to seep through to one," so that all actions are tempered by a sub-text, though obvious to everyone, a strategy which the author claimed to have discovered when he delivered his Fisk University oration.

Whenever the narrator questions his mother about racial relationships, she is defensive and evasive. "I knew there was something my mother was holding back," he notes. "She was not concealing facts, but feelings, attitudes, convictions which she did not want me to know," a misrepresentation which disturbs "black boy" who later says "my personality was lopsided; my knowledge of feeling was far greater than my knowledge of fact." While he holds back or conceals facts, he is usually straightforward about emotional feelings, even though he can say "the safety of my life in the South depended upon how well I concealed from all whites what I felt." Worrying less about factual truth, Wright was determined to stress the emotional truth of Southern life to counteract the stereotypical myths shown in the song which prefaced *Uncle Tom's Children:* "Is it true what they say about Dixie? Does the sun really shine all the time?"

One of the particular ironies of *Black Boy* is that the narrator's constant lying is emblematic of the truth that all black boys were required not only to lie, but to lie about their lying. In the boxing match between "black boy" and a co-worker, this pattern is played out almost mathematically. The two black boys are coerced into a fight . . . based on lies that are obvious to all. Much of the shamefulness of the whole situation is that they are forced to pretend that they are neither aware that the situation is false, nor that they know the whites know they know. . . . Although personal and institutional racism was everywhere evident, Southern whites generally maintained that they treated blacks more humanely than did Northern whites, that they understood blacks and knew how to deal with them, and that they were friendly with blacks (as evidenced by their calling them by their first names), all of which blacks were supposed to pretend they believed. Whites deliberately set up situations where blacks were forced to steal, and not only did they like to be stolen from, they forced blacks to lie by repeatedly asking them if they were thieves. "Whites placed a premium upon black deceit; they encouraged irresponsibility; and their rewards were bestowed upon us blacks in the degree that we could make them feel safe and superior," notes the narrator. When "black boy" forgets to call a white coworker named Pease "Mister," he is caught in a trap from which the usual escape is "a nervous cryptic smile." The boy's attempt to lie his way out of the situation fails, despite his ingenuity in turning the false accusation into an ambiguous apology: . . .

"I don't remember calling you *Pease*, Mr. Pease," I said cautiously.

"And if I did, I sure didn't mean . . ."

"You black sonofabitch! You called me *Pease*, then!" he spat, rising and slapping me till I bent sideways over a bench.

Episodes like this make clear that inability to tell the truth does not make black boys into liars. Instead the frequent descriptions of the protagonist as a prevaricator reveal to white readers the way blacks used lies as express truths, used, for example, the word "nigger" to mean one thing to white listeners, another to black. The elaborate system of signifying, of using words exactly the opposite of white usage (bad for good/cool for hot), of wearing the mask to cover emotions, of the lies behind black children's game of dozens—all of these are behind the motif of lying in *Black Boy*. Wright's metaphoric use of lying is made more complex by his awareness that a history of misrepresentation of true feelings made it difficult for black people to be certain when they were merely dissembling for protection, when they were lying to each other, or to themselves. "There are some elusive, profound, recondite things that men find hard to say to other men," muses "black boy," "but with the Negro it is the little things of life that become hard to say, for these tiny items shape his destiny." What sets him apart from his contemporaries is his difficulty with the lying they find so easy: "In my dealing with whites I was conscious of the entirety of my relations with them, and they were conscious only of what was happening at a given moment. I had to keep remembering what others took for granted; I had to think out what others felt."

The actual audience must narrow the gap between the narrative and authorial audience; the reader of *Black Boy* must strive to be like the narrator of *Black Boy*, must keep what is happening at a particular moment and the entire history of black/white relations—the content and the context—together in his or her mind. Wright's context includes the need to speak simultaneously as an adult and as a child, to remove everything from his story that, even if it happened to be true, would allow white readers to maintain their distorted stereotype of Southern blacks. He was searching for a way to confess his personal history of lying, forced on him by his childhood, while still demonstrating that he could be trusted by both black and white. . . .

BLACK BOY REMAINS NARRATIVE TRUTH

Black Boy should not be read as historical truth which strives to report those incontrovertible facts that can be somehow corroborated, but as narrative truth, which psychiatrist Donald Spence defines as "the criterion we use to decide when a certain experience has been captured to our satisfaction; it depends on continuity and closure and the extent to which the fit of the pieces takes on an aesthetic finality." The story that Richard Wright creates in *Black Boy*, whatever its value as an exact historical record, is important both in telling us how the author remembers life in the pre-Depression South and in showing us what kind of person the author was to have written his story as he did. Although he is often deliberately false to historical truth, he seldom deviates from narrative truth. "Consistent misrepresentation of oneself is not easy," writes Roy Pascal, and in *Black Boy* Wright has made both the horrifying dramatic and the ordinary events of his life fit into a pattern, shaped by a consistent, metaphoric use of lying. "Interpretations are persuasive," argues Donald Spence, "not because of their evidential value but because their rhetorical appeal; conviction emerges because the fit is good, not because we have necessarily made contact with the past."

In *Black Boy* Wright creates a version of himself whose metaphor for survival and for sustenance is falsehood. But the multiple lies of the narrator, like the fibs of children trying to avoid what they see as irrational punishment, are palpably obvious. They are not meant to deceive; they are deliberately embarrassing in their transparency. For the protagonist, whose home life was so warped that only when he lied could he be believed, Alfred Kazin's dictum—"One writes to make a home for oneself, on paper"—is particularly true. The author's manipulations of genre and his metaphoric lies produced a book about which Du Bois's assessment was, in my judgment, exactly backward: although much of what Wright wrote is not literally true, the total picture is ultimately convincing, taken in context. For all his lying, "black boy's" essential drive is for truth, and his constant revelation of how often he was forced to lie should be judged according to the standard set forth by Marcel Eck in *Lies and Truth*: "We will be judged not on whether we possess or do not possess the truth but on whether or not we sought and loved it."

CHAPTER 2

Themes and Metaphor in *Black Boy*

Writing as Survival in *Black Boy*

Joseph T. Skerrett Jr.

Joseph T. Skerrett Jr., associate professor of English at the University of Massachusetts in Amherst, explains how the lack of trust Wright felt first within his own family and later in the community made him feel like a person who was "dead in life," someone who could not initiate action or control the events of his surroundings. Through his writing, however, Wright survived this living death, discovering the personal usefulness of literature as it formed his identity as a writer and a man.

Richard Wright's imagination internalized and absorbed, with deadly fascination, "the white death"—the Mississippi environment of terror, which constantly threatened him. In *Black Boy* he notes that "tension would set in at the mere mention of whites and a vast complex of emotions, involving the whole of my personality, would be aroused. It was as though I was continuously reacting to the threat of some natural force whose hostile behavior could not be predicted. I had never in my life been abused by whites, but I had already become as conditioned to their existence as though I had been the victim of a thousand lynchings." Wright's response to this deeply felt anxiety and fear of death is analogous to the psychological responses of the Hiroshima victims studied by Robert Jay Lifton in *History and Human Survival.* Lifton himself gives sanction for the use of his work's insights in other contexts when he says "In light of the Hiroshima experience we should also consider the possibility that in other disasters or extreme situations there may also be more significant inner encounters with death, immediate or longer-term, than we have heretofore supposed." As Richard Wright experienced it, "the white death"

Excerpted from Joseph T. Skerrett Jr., "Richard Wright: Writing and Identity," *Callaloo*, vol. 2, no. 3 (October 1979), pp. 84–93, 124. Copyright © 1979 Charles H. Rowell. Reprinted by permission of the Johns Hopkins University Press. (Footnotes in the original have been omitted in this reprint.)

was just such an "extreme situation," permanently altering conceptions and emotional responses to matters of life and death. . . .

A WORLD WITHOUT TRUST

As *Black Boy* witnesses, trust had never been very firmly established in Wright's world of experience. With undeniable deliberateness, *Black Boy* gives the reader a strong impression of life in a virtually loveless family. Particularly conspicuous by its absence is the memory of paternal love and affection; even before his abandonment of his family, when Richard was about four years old, Nathaniel Wright seems to have cast only an emotionally pale shadow in his son's direction.

Wright's biographer, Michel Fabre, notes that Wright came early "to regard his father solely as an incarnation of authority, which his own weakness prevented him from escaping, and in no way saw him as an example to follow or a figure to be proud of and love." The father provided no ego-ideal for the son; furthermore, he did not build upon his paternal authority. The first incident reported in *Black Boy*, young Richard's half-accidental burning of the house, concludes with a severe punishment administered by his mother, though his father is present throughout. Later Richard confronts his father's emotionless role as "the lawgiver in [the] family . . . a stranger . . . always somehow alien and remote." He literally interprets his father's angry response to a noisy stray kitten and kills it, thus confounding his father's authority. Again it is his mother who administers the punishment, evoking guilt and fear of vengeance from God for the child's cruel treatment of the kitten. Not much later, Nathaniel Wright left his wife and two young sons for another woman. In young Richard's now fatherless world, the censorious and disciplinary role was permanently transferred from the male to the females in his family—to his mother and to his grandmother and aunts. . . .

While Richard lived with his mother and younger brother in his grandmother's household, they all struggled against her puritanical Seventh Day Adventist religiosity. Grandmother Wilson's daily prayer routines, "her fiat that day began at sunrise and that night commenced at sundown," the lengthy Bible readings, the observance of the Holy Sabbath on Saturday (so that Richard could not work for pocket money like other kids), all produced tension, bickering and recrimination. At school, where his youngest aunt, Addie, was briefly his teacher, Richard's situation was no better. He received a beating from Addie because the young teacher wanted to make an impression on the class. When Addie tried to continue the beating at home, Richard defended himself with a knife; they struggled "like strangers, deadly enemies . . . kicking, scratching, hitting, fighting." There were, Wright remembered, "more violent quarrels in our deeply religious home than in the home of a gangster, a burglar, or a prostitute."

His rejection of family direction left Wright socially uncertain, distrustful and insecure. This basic insecurity was reinforced when Wright's mother found it necessary to lodge him temporarily in an orphanage; he learned rapidly there, he reports, to "distrust everything and everybody" and became aware of himself as an individual pitched in conflict with all others. His early life had failed to give him the kind of support necessary to reinforce the sense of basic trust which Erik Erikson argues is established at the mother's breast. We cannot know whether Wright as an infant negotiated *that* crisis successfully. But we do know that he never made the transfer of faith and trust from mother to the related "institutionalized endeavor of man—religion," Erikson says. Throughout his life, a large part of the traditional matrix of support in his community—the church—was thus unavailable, alienated from and useless to him.

The racial threat to life in Mississippi only served to exacerbate and reinforce this alienation from familial and cultural reducers of tension. Indeed, early in his life—by the age of sixteen or so, according to Saunders Redding—Wright had learned both experientially and intellectually that "the white death" had already reached him, that he was already— by virtue of having been born black—cast among the living dead. Whites treated all blacks, he discovered, as if they were objects, not persons. "As a hotel bellboy in a Southern town he had been summoned to rooms where naked white women lolled about unmoved by any sense of shame at his presence," as if he were invisible or non-existent. And he had by that time already read William James, who gave him what Redding calls "objective philosophical confirmation of his experiences." In Wright's "Introduction" to Horace Cayton's and St. Clair Drake's *Black Metropolis*, the following passage from James (which Redding argues is central to Wright's understanding of the racial terror) is quoted:

> A man has as many social selves as there are individuals who recognize him and carry an image of him in their minds. . . . No more fiendish punishment could be devised, were such a thing possible, than that one should be turned loose in society and remain absolutely unnoticed by all the members thereof. If no one turned round when we entered, answered when we spoke, or minded what we did, but if every person we met "cut us dead" and acted as if we were non-existent things, a kind of rage and impotent despair would long well up in us, from which the cruelest bodily tortures would be a relief; for those would make us feel that, however bad might be our plight, we had not sunk to such a depth as to be unworthy of attention at all.

Contemplating this living death, this total negation of one's personal existence as a sensate human being, Wright, very much like the Hiroshima victims in Lifton's studies, focused his imagination on a single incident or aspect of the total experience. This "one ultimate horror" then came to epitomize the death-centered environment.

ULTIMATE HORROR

For Wright, that key event among the multiple horrors was lynching. In *Black Boy* he indicates his response upon being told of the castration and murder of a young man he had known. This young man had, allegedly, been sleeping with a white prostitute in a hotel where he worked as a bellhop: "What I had heard altered the look of the world, induced in me a temporary paralysis of will and impulse. The penalty of death awaited me if I made a false move and I wondered if it was worthwhile to make any move at all." The threat of death embodied in this ultimate and unremediable news became a symbol to Wright of his condemnation to existence as a person-dead-in-life, unable to initiate action or to control events:

> The things that influenced my conduct as a Negro did not have to happen to me directly; I needed but to hear of them to feel their full effect in the deepest layer of my consciousness. Indeed the white brutality that I had not seen was a more effective control of my behavior than that which I knew. . . . As long as it remained something terrible and yet remote, something whose horror and blood might descend upon me at any moment, I was compelled to give my entire imagination over to it, an act which blocked the springs of thought and feeling in me, creating a sense of distance between me and the world in which I lived.

Wright's most successful published poem, entitled "Between
the World and Me," reiterates this association of terror and
personal alienation in the face of the threat of castration and
death in a lynch mob's hands. The voice of the observer, in
this poem, is that of an innocent but imaginative and sensitive youth. "One morning while in the woods," he stumbles
upon the "sooty details" of a lynching scene. The pastoral
calm of the "scaly oaks and elms" stands in stark contrast to
the human debris: "a vacant shoe, an empty tie, a ripped
shirt, a lonely hat and a pair of trousers stiff with black
blood." And as the sun "poured yellow surprise" into the
staring eyes of "a stony skull," the observer is "frozen with a
cold pity for the life that was gone." As the observer's imagination is gripped by the scene, the bright morning vanishes;
it is night and "the grey ashes" of the lynched man rise,
forming "flesh firm and black," entering into, merging with,
becoming the speaker's own body. The speaker undergoes
the terror and the pain of the actual lynching whose site he
had stumbled upon in his walk through the woods. The
rhythms of the verses are strong, powerful in their pace and
stroke; the images are so vividly kinesthetic that the reader
shares in the observer's physical agony as he is transformed
into the lynching victim:

> And then they had me, stripped me battering my teeth
> into my throat till I swallowed my own blood.
> My voice was drowned in the roar of their own voices,
> and my black wet body slipped and rolled in their
> hands as they bound me to the sapling.

Doused first by a "baptism of gasoline," the victim/observer
expires amidst the flames as the pain rises "like water."
"Clutched to the hot sides of death," his agony is complete.
Now it is the reader who has come out of his innocent wood-
side to spy "dry bones" and "a stony skull staring in /
yellow surprise at the sun. . . ."

Between the world and Richard Wright there always lay
the ambiguous shadow of the racial situation in all its his-
toric and psychological dimensions. The association of
lynchings and other mob violence by whites against blacks
with the anti-miscegenation taboos of Dixie society is strong
in Wright's early stories and in *Black Boy*. The act of aggression against women, then, becomes in his psychological
makeup doubly-charged; there is at once this manifest racial
pressure coming from Southern society with its threat of

castration and death standing behind a general denial of personhood, and the guilt accruing from his long-suppressed desire to strike out at women in his family—his emotionally unresponsive mother, aunts, and grandmother.

A RESTLESS LONELINESS

In *Black Boy* Wright is conspicuously reticent about his relations with women outside of his family. But in another autobiographical fragment, published as "Early Days in Chicago" in 1945 and as "The Man Who Went to Chicago" in the posthumous *Eight Men* of 1961, he reveals, I believe, a transfer of his family problem to a social context. In the fragment he describes a period of his life spent as an insurance collector among poor blacks in the Chicago slums. He had been lying with one young woman in exchange for his payment of the ten-cent weekly premium on her policy. One day in conversation she noted that Jim, another young man of her intimate acquaintance, was more "fun" to be with. Wright, moved to jealousy, asked her why she was with him at all if she liked Jim so much.

> "You all right," she said, giggling. "I like you."
> "I could kill you," I said.
> "What?" she said.
> "Nothing," I said, ashamed.
> "Kill me, you said? You crazy, man," she said.
> "Maybe I am," I muttered, angry that I was sitting beside a human being to whom I could not talk, angry with myself for coming to her, hating my wild and restless loneliness.

The "wild and restless loneliness" was there in his personality from his youth until his last days; it deeply affected his relationships with others—and with women in particular. It is inextricably entangled with his experience of fatherlessness and the astringent, emotionally unfulfilling relationships with the women of his family. In his dealing with the young women in Chicago, these themes make themselves manifest in a social setting outside the family; the girl's preference for Jim makes him feel inadequate and inferior. He desires to make his rejection of her clear and even final; he needs to assert his mastery over the limiting and censorious female by striking back in violence, by "killing."

This behavior represents a vigorous rejection of the negative identity thrust upon him by both family and society and, as such, is a radical departure from the morphology of the survivor that I have been tracing in Wright's development.

Unlike many of Wright's black neighbors in Mississippi, he did not succumb to the temptation of *psychic numbing* that Lifton speaks of as characteristic of such negative peak-experiences. Lifton argues, "human beings are unable to remain open to emotional experience ... for any length of time, and very quickly ... there begins to occur what we may term psychic closing-off [later *psychic numbing*], that is, people simply cease to feel."

Certainly, Wright saw plenty of this in those around him. As Ralph Ellison makes clear, there were essentially three ways of handling one's black destiny in the South of Richard Wright's youth. One could retreat into religion, as Wright's family to a great degree did, and resign oneself to the way things were in this world. Seeing the racial situation *sub specie aeternitas* [forever unequal], one would then await justice beyond the grave and believe that those who came into open conflict with the whites were evil people, predestined for failure and punishment. Or, one would repress his hatred of the Jim Crow laws and other forms of racial subjugation and strive ceaselessly for middle-class status and bourgeois respectability—freedom from the share-cropping cycle, a college education for his children, a share in the American dream.

Both of these methods of dealing with the problem involve considerable degrees of psychic numbing: in the face of "the white death" (recurrent beatings, rapes, lynchings and insults as well as legal inequities, employment and educational discrimination, and inferior living conditions) members of the black community who had chosen one or the other of these positions were forced to prevent themselves from feeling that overwhelming negation of their existence, which William James described as being "cut dead" by society and which Richard Wright felt as the overwhelming fact of his being-in-the-world.

Almost everyone in the black community had chosen one or the other of these routes—or some amalgam of the two—and the black community cooperated to make the one-eyed view of reality inherent in them the only view of reality that could be obtained. Thus the kind of rebellion that Wright's attitudes embodied seemed criminal, "sinful"—and, ultimately, dangerous to the safety of the entire community. One major technique used by Mississippi blacks to control potential rebels was the system of warm personal relations that prevailed within the community. But just as Wright came to feel the lash of violence from the hand of the loving mother, he also came intuitively to understand the ambiguity of interpersonal relations in the shadow of the white death:

> After the habit of reflection had been born in me, I used to mull over the strange absence of real kindness in Negroes, how unstable was our tenderness, how lacking in genuine passion we were, how void of great hope, how timid our joy, how bare our traditions, how hollow our memories, how lacking we were in those intangible sentiments that bind man to man, and how shallow was even our despair. . . . I saw that what we had taken for our emotional strength was our negative confusion, our flights, our fears, our frenzy under pressure.

The strategies of the community, so deeply infused with psychological self-denial, self-hatred, and what Lifton terms in his Hiroshima survivors *psychic numbing,* force its members to fear the emotional investment of tenderness. The white death turns the community's resentment and frenzy against the rebels within, who threaten the safety of all by questioning the emotional anaesthesia of the community stances. Thus the slap in the face Wright received from his mother when he innocently asked why the blacks did not strike back at the white terrorists who had killed his uncle is, in effect, a stroke of community self-defense, a perverted act of tenderness and concern, designed to block the potential rebel from further acts of madness or "sin."

A REBEL IN THE FACE OF DEATH

Only such a rebel can look into the face of the white death and not be psychologically blinded by the vision of unpredictable and everlasting horror he sees there. Once again like the Hiroshima survivors, Richard Wright experienced shame and guilt when he contemplated his brutalized condition. In *Black Boy* he tells how fear kept him from speaking when asked by his white employer which of his white fellow-workers had threatened him:

> I stared ahead of me and did not answer. He waved the men aside. The white stenographer looked at me with wide eyes and I felt drenched in shame, naked to my soul. The whole of my being felt violated, and I knew that my own fear had helped to violate it.

And this reaction he saw as central to the experience of all who shared in black life, all who shared his subjugated existence. In *12,000,000 Black Voices* he spoke of the feeling in the communal plural:

> We contemplate our lack of courage in the face of daily force,
> we are seized with a desire to escape our shameful identifi-
> cation. . . .

Wright rejected the anaesthesia of the emotions which
made these survival methods practicable, and chose instead
the role and route of the rebel. Ralph Ellison describes this
third way of dealing with one's black destiny as adopting
criminality and carrying on "an unceasing scrimmage with
the whites, which often flared forth into physical violence.". . . But in his own case there was an important difference: Richard Wright wanted to do something more than defend his personal integrity in the racial wilderness. *His*
rebellion he wanted to distribute to the masses of his oppressed fellow blacks. His flight to Chicago was survival motion at its most basic; he could not fulfill himself in the atmosphere of his family or in the milieu of Mississippi. But
no more in his life than in his work is mere flight a central
theme. Having examined his early years and his development of an individualistic consciousness in the face of familial and societal opposition, he asked himself how it happened: "From where in this southern darkness had I caught
a sense of freedom? . . . What was it that made me feel things
deeply enough for me to try to order my life by my feelings?"
Literature was his answer. In his estimation, it had been literature that had nurtured his sense of freedom. And it would
be in literature that he would attempt to work out the tangled skein of his private and social feelings. . . .

In *Black Boy* he tells us that he discovered the personal
usefulness of literature as a result of reading an editorial attack on H.L. Mencken in a Memphis newspaper.

> The only people I had ever heard denounced in the South
> were Negroes, and this man was not a Negro. Then what
> ideas did Mencken hold that made a newspaper like the *Com-
> mercial Appeal* castigate him publicly? . . . I felt a vague sym-
> pathy for him. Had not the South, which had assigned me the
> role of a non-man, cast at him its harshest words?

As he read Mencken's works he discovered support for his
own distrustful dissenting attitudes toward the institutions
that hemmed his spirit in. Mencken attacked and satirized
"the weakness of people . . . God, authority;" in Mencken he
found a fellow rebel, a man who used words as his weapons,
wielded them "as one would use a club." A latent creative
faculty was aroused by this element of overt social criticism:

"the impulse to dread had been slowly beaten out of me by experience. Now it surged up again and I hungered for books, new ways of looking and seeing."

The insights of literature were, of course, not the exclusive property of H.L. Mencken. Wright also read, with care, the works of Sinclair Lewis, Edgar Allan Poe, Gertrude Stein, Sherwood Anderson, Stephen Crane, Joseph Conrad, Theodore Dreiser, John Dos Passos, and James T. Farrell.

The human content of these modern writers gave Wright new views on the structure of the world, on language, on social consciousness, on history. His aggressive and rebellious drives were reinforced by the new stimuli, and with the resurgence of these long-suppressed drives, Wright experienced a renewal of guilt feelings. Some of these feelings were related to race and Southern society:

> Reading was like a drug, a dope. The novels created moods in which I lived for days. But I could not conquer my sense of guilt, my feeling that the white men around me knew I was changing, that I had begun to regard them differently.

Other feelings of guilt arose from his now quickened consciousness of his relationships within the family; "Dreiser's *Jennie Gerhards* and *Sister Carrie* revived in [him] a vivid sense of [his] mother's suffering."

Thus, the act of writing, a revived impulse to which followed shortly upon this period of intensified reading, was invested with the patterns of guilt and aggression that *Black Boy* reports in Wright's early life. It was the critical, satiric elements in Mencken, Dreiser, Farrell and the other writers that first attracted Wright, for they provided him with mechanisms for the "outering" of his burdensome internal tensions—both familial/sexual and racial/social (with all their inevitable and unavoidable interrelationships). His reading gave him a sense of a meaningful, emotionally free, expressive life: "All my life," he tells us in *Black Boy* "had shaped me for the realism, the naturalism of the modern novel." The novels he read and his frustrating early efforts to write created tensions of their own—"new, terrible, surging, almost too great to be contained"—for both served to clarify and reinforce his perceptions of his situation: "I no longer felt that the world about me was hostile, killing; I *knew* it. A million times I asked myself what I could do to save myself, and there were no answers. I seem forever condemned, ringed by walls."

Wright spent his entire creative life ringed by this tension. As Constance Webb has recorded in her biography, Wright sat to each new writing project in a palpable knot of tension, for his identity as a "sensate human being," a real person, capable of initiating meaningful action, capable of bringing possibilities to fruition, capable of something *more* than survival motion, was placed on the line with every new composition. . . . Wright's struggle with his identity as a human person is inextricable from his activity as, a writer; his writing was a complex, therapeutic "outering" of his psychosocial burdens. The tension of trust/distrust between the world and him, engendered in the family environment and nurtured by a racist society, was reduced but never removed either by writing or by exile. When he laid his burden down in 1960, he was at work on a novel dealing with an alienated black Mississippian's experiences among both black and white American *emigrés* in Paris.

Richard Wright: The Self and the South

William L. Andrews

William L. Andrews is professor of English at the University of Wisconsin, Madison, and the author of *To Tell a Free Story: The First Century of Afro-American Autobiography, 1760–1865.* Andrews writes that Wright's autobiography sends a double message of optimism and skepticism about black southerners' ability to achieve a full sense of identity in America. Wright, however, as demonstrated in *Black Boy*, does discover liberating ways to identity himself as a writer, a southerner, and an American.

Mississippi recognized selfhood not as a function of the subject but of the object, namely the racial other, whose looming presence dictated the need for self-differentiation according *to* the strictures of law and custom rather than in creative opposition to them. What happens, however, when the southern youth discovers that the law is not a single but a double standard? This introduces the problem, among black southerners especially, of how to identify with half a society without feeling oneself to be but half a person. Among modern white southern autobiographers, the problem of identity is similarly one of incompleteness, symbolized by a sense of unresolved conflict within the self over one's attitude toward blacks. . . .

The fundamental difference that the southern system of social difference makes in much modern autobiography from the South is this: it makes the notion of individuation—the achievement of personal indivisibility—a persistent, though not always recognized or acknowledged, ideal. . . .

DISCOVERING THE DIFFERENCE

When Wright discovered the difference that whiteness makes, the structure and order of all his relationships, with

Excerpted from William L. Andrews, "In Search of a Common Identity: The Self and the South in Four Mississippi Writers," *The Southern Review*, vol. 24, no. 1 (Winter 1988), pp. 47–64. Reprinted by permission of the author.

his family as well as his community, are undermined. On a train ride to Arkansas, young Richard tries to understand what gives white people their special status in the railroad station and on the cars. The problem leads him to probe the significance of whiteness itself. He asks his mother whether his grandmother, who looks white to him, is a white woman. If so, then why does she associate with colored people like himself? Did she "'become colored when she married Grandpa?" Is whiteness acquired or innate? Receiving no clear answers from his evasive, increasingly defensive mother, the boy tries to penetrate the mystery by tracing his grandmother's origins, but this only leads him to a blank, an unnamed and unknown white great-grandfather. Why does whiteness signify absence for some white people while conferring status on others? Who makes the decision, and why will "they" call him "a colored man" when he grows up, regardless of the whiteness in his own heritage? Concluding that his mother is trying to "shut [him] out of the secret," Richard, already troubled by a sense of alienation from his family, feels all the more alone and powerless. Without answers to the secret of the world's arbitrary, capricious, and repressive power over him, he barricades himself in the world of his own imagination and sustains himself on fantasies of violent reprisal against the motiveless malignity of whiteness. As narrator, Wright observes that the "emotional integrity" he developed as a child was an outgrowth of these fantasies. Eventually, though "I had never in my life been abused by whites," "at the mere mention of whites" "a vast complex of emotions, involving the whole of my personality, would be aroused," out of which young Richard created "a culture, a creed, a religion." In one sense *Black Boy* is the story of Wright's progress from his boyish fantasies of a desperate integrity based on rebellion against the terrible other to an ideal of selfhood liberated from an opposition to otherness as its negative *raison d' être.*

In *Black Boy* whiteness alone does not comprise the totality of repressive forces that Richard must resist. The first half of the book emphasizes the conformity that black authority, whether familial or institutional, demands from the black boy. Wright says he rejected the black males on whom he might have modeled himself because they seemed obsessed with forcing him to accept a place in a pecking order, rather than encouraging him to discover who he was. As a boy the only way Wright could express his desire for authenticity was through acts of verbal aggression, in which he persistently offended his elders' sense of dignity and propriety by speaking and writing "dirty words." As a teenager Wright encoded his resistance to white authority in speech acts that seemed to him unprovocative but were in fact just as much a profanation of the rituals of caste intercourse as the boy's obscenities were of his black elders' dignity. This is what his friend Griggs recognizes when he warns Wright, "You act around white people as if you didn't know that they were white. And they *see* it." Motivating all this offensive behavior toward others, Wright explains, was a fundamental need throughout his youth to view his world wholly, as a community, and to negotiate his world not through images and roles but as an authentic personality. "It was simply utterly impossible for me to calculate, to scheme, to act. . . . I would remember to dissemble for short periods, then I would forget and act straight and human again, not with the desire to harm anybody, but merely forgetting the artificial status of race and class. It was the same with whites as with blacks; it was my way with everybody."

It would be more accurate, in light of what is narrated in *Black Boy*, to say that this was Wright's *preferred* way with everybody. Very little in his description of his dealings with whites and blacks during his crucial last two years in the South suggests that he had any real hope of finding an alternative to the image and role of "non-man" that the caste system expected of him. The extreme hostility and humiliation that he suffers while trying to "work his way up" in a Jackson, Mississippi, optical shop leaves him feeling profoundly "violated," "slapped out of the human race." Even though his boss, Mr. Crane, apparently sympathetic to the black youth, asks Wright to tell him what happened, Wright refuses. "There's no use of my saying anything." Gradually the youth whose principal weapon against the world had been words begins to fall silent, the ultimate sign, in Wright's case, of his alienation from his southern environment. The last chapters of *Black Boy* record his consistent refusal to talk to any whites, even to a solicitous Yankee like Falk, the bookish Irishman, "hated by the white Southerners," who might have shared much with Wright. While the black youth accepts the white man's library card, which gives him illicit access to the Memphis library, he spurns his benefactor's in-

vitation to discuss with him his reactions to the works of
Mencken, Dreiser, and other American realist novelists. "It
would have meant talking about myself and that would have
been too painful." There is no more despairing depiction of
the inhibition of other-confrontation and self-revelation in
modern southern autobiography than this.

WRIGHT'S NEW IDENTITIES

Nevertheless, out of this seeming ratification of unbridge-
able difference emerges, in the climax of *Black Boy*, the
alienated black youth's discovery of new, potentially liberating ways of identifying himself as a writer, a southerner, and
an American. The loss of the hope of community within the
narrow boundaries of caste relationships, where so little can
be spoken safely, provokes and actually facilitates Wright's
search for "a world elsewhere" (to use Richard Poirier's
phrase), not just in the magical land of "the North," but in
the idealized unboundedness of the written word. Thus
when young Wright encounters the combative literary style
of *Prejudices*, he imagines himself, however doubtfully, as
another Mencken, "using words as a weapon" against injustice. Through Dreiser's Carrie Meeber and Jennie Gerhardt,
he recovers from the past "a vivid sense of my mother's suffering." After finishing *Main Street* and *Babbitt*, he no longer
views his pretentious white boss, Mr. Gerald, as quite the
implacable and inexplicable other. "I felt that I knew him"
and could "identify him as an American type." In short,
Wright's retreat into the world of literature does not seal his
alienation; it liberates him from it by enhancing his powers
of imaginative identification. He begins to recognize himself
in and *through* others, even the once terrible other, by way
of their common Americanness as revealed in the national
perspective of the American realist novel. What he had been
rebelling against in the South he understands as part of a
larger "straitened American environment," that writers, indeed *white* writers, were trying to reshape "nearer to the
hearts of those who lived in it." In this community the black
man from the South believes he can become a self-wrighter.

Richard Wright acknowledges in the last paragraphs of
Black Boy that he did not go north with an integral sense of
the self he wanted to become. He went to Chicago "running
more away from something than toward something." Anyone who reads *American Hunger* (1977), the posthumously

THE CONCEPT OF DIFFERENCE

Andrews explains that caste and class difference has been important to southern social and economic systems throughout its history.

The concept of difference, of course, is crucial to southern notions of corporate identity. The feudal South fought the Civil War out of a conviction that it was a social, economic, and cultural entity different from the North and ought to be granted its political independence from Yankeedom as well. After that debacle, southern white writers could be expected to make much of their region's spiritual differences from the rest of the Union, portraying Dixie as "a special redemptive community fulfilling a divinely appointed role in the drama of history." Black southerners inherited from their oppressed ancestors an image of themselves as a chosen people too, though it took a Martin Luther King, Jr., to make temporally viable the traditional black belief in a corporate apotheosis in the hereafter. George Brown Tindall reminds us that during times of national crisis in the twentieth century, southern blacks and whites have vied with each other for the right to proclaim themselves alone the guardians of true Americanism.

Caste and class difference has also been the key to southern social and economic structures throughout its history. The segregation system that evolved after the Civil War was founded on the assumption of essential genetic differences between whites and blacks and ineradicable social gradations among whites. The idea of Jim Crow was to regulate all dealings between the races so that the difference between white status and black status would be consistently attested and publicly confirmed. Caste solidarity was enforced among both whites and blacks, ostensibly out of each community's desire for self-preservation, but also because of fear and distrust of the racial other, into which each caste could project its fantasies and/or its repressed negative imagery of itself. Each caste tended to interpret any member's deviations from prescribed behavior simply as a sign of caste disloyalty: thus, white individualists could be impugned as "nigger lovers" for a wide range of social infractions, while individualistic blacks were condemned, often by both castes, for "trying to be white." Southern behavior exhibited many characteristics of what Erik Erikson has called the "ideological mind," typical of a people preoccupied, as an adolescent is, by peer approval and confirmation of one's worth by creeds and rituals that simultaneously furnish assurance that what is different is alien and inimical.

William L. Andrews, "In Search of a Common Identity: The Self and the South in Four Mississippi Writers," *Southern Review*, vol. 24, no. 1, Winter 1988, p. 49.

published sequel to *Black Boy*, knows that Wright did not find the community, in personal, political, or artistic terms, that he vaguely imagined lay beyond his southern horizons in 1927. Wright's autobiographies testify eloquently to his hunger for an identity realized in community, but they do not picture his achievement of a communal identity in an historically locatable place and time. Wright's autobiographies send a double message, therefore, of optimism and skepticism about the possibility of the black southerner's achieving a fulfilling sense of identity and community in America. The experience of Richard Wright *within* history, as history is reconstructed in his autobiographies, justifies the skepticism that Morris reported in Wright's conversation with him—namely, that black children could not expect to grow up in America "as human beings." Yet the voice of Richard Wright as narrator in the timeless world of his text engages his American reader in a community of intimate discourse that is plainly intended to defy history, the very history that Wright claims to have personally experienced, in which all such efforts to engage the other in community are frustrated. As a result of the dialectical relationship of the voice of community and the experience of history in *Black Boy*, the reader is forced to make a choice of identification between one of two Richard Wrights.

The Strength of Individual Will

Donald B. Gibson

Donald B. Gibson, professor of English at Rutgers
University and widely published scholar of African
American studies, describes how Wright asserted his
individual will in the household that rejected him
and learned to become a self-reliant individual.
Black Boy, Gibson says, is Wright's chronicle of this
growth and his struggle to resist the authority of his
community as he strove to distance himself from
negative influences in his environment.

The stuff of Richard Wright's *Black Boy* originates from his
experience of life in the South, in Mississippi, Arkansas, and
Tennessee. The shape of the work, however, derives from
Wright's experience in the North; for the autobiography's
retrospective character allowed Wright to imagine that his
early experience was preparing him to be the person he
found himself to be after he had been in Chicago and New
York for some years. It is from that perspective that the earlier events of his life are narrated, and it is because of that
perspective that Wright chooses what events from his past to
relate and how to relate them.

ASSERTING AN INDIVIDUAL WILL

It is also because of the perspective from which the autobiography is written that there are several inconsistencies between his own account and that of Michel Fabre in his definitive biography. For example, in his actual life as a youth
Wright had several close friends, but his *Black Boy* describes
none of these relationships. The sense we get of his family's
actual social standing in their community as told in the biography is not revealed in the autobiography. These discrepancies exist because Wright conceived his experience from

Excerpted from Donald B. Gibson, "Richard Wright's *Black Boy* and the Trauma of Au-
tobiographical Rebirth," *Callaloo*, vol. 9, no. 3 (Summer 1986), pp. 492–94, 496–99.
Copyright © 1986 Charles H. Rowell. Reprinted by permission of the Johns Hopkins
University Press.

109

his birth to the time he composed *Black Boy* as a description
of one who from his very earliest times was a strong individualist. Hence his very first memory, the memory of setting fire to his family's house, is of an act of defiance and ex-
ertion of individual will. That he sets the house on fire is not
entirely an accident, for he seems old enough to know what
is going to happen if he puts flame to the "fluffy white curtains" which he has specifically been forbidden by his parents to touch. His description of the act begins the autobiography because it is to him emblematic of his essential
character: he is the strong individualist capable initially of
defying parental authority at the cost nearly of death ("my
mother had come close to killing me"), and eventually of defying the authority of the whole southern institutional
scheme. Significantly enough the beating he receives at the
beginning of the autobiography is administered by his
mother, and the instrument with which he is chastised is not
a switch, but a "tree limb." He is in a fevered and hysterical
state for several days, suggesting that the beating was rather
severe. That initial scene tells us not only that he is strong
enough even at four years of age to defy parental authority,
but, as well, it indicates intense emotional disruption of the
ordinarily sympathetic bond between parent and child, especially mother and child. Whether in actual fact his life was
in danger or whether his reaction was a hysterical reaction
to the extraordinarily harsh beating he received at the hands
of his mother, the fact is that he felt as though his mother,
whom the child expected to protect, nourish, and sustain his
life, came close to expressing the most extreme form of rejection—infanticide. The whole of the autobiography's first
chapter is centered around the failure of his parents to fulfill the parental role. It begins by illustrating how the mother
has failed him, and it ends by showing how the father has
failed him and failed in life as well. Clearly Wright's father,
the logic goes, was not a good model to emulate. Each section of the first chapter reveals another facet of Wright's parents' failing him or his assuming himself functions originally belonging to them. The point is that failing to find the
necessary support and sustaining function in adults or in a
community, he had to rely upon himself—to cultivate those
qualities in himself, to become self-reliant, a strong individualist. That is why in the book Wright differs from every
other black person who appears in that world. And that is

why he is able to resist efforts on the parts of black and white alike to make him conform to an inimical scheme of values. . . .

The burden of the whole of the first chapter of *Black Boy* is a recital of examples of parental rejection providing an explanation and a justification for Wright's individualism. Once the individual severs himself from his family life, his disaffection from the community may likely follow. Wright's logic proceeds along these lines: he explains his individualism, his separateness, by reference to the character of his early life. "How could I have turned out differently?" his narration asks. It tells us that there is no way he could have been different; no way he could have done otherwise than to cut himself off from community. His parents fail him utterly. The greatness of the narration of the autobiography lies in Wright's dual awareness of the nature of the failure: it is personal; it is social. It has to do with the personalities of his parents; it has to do with the situation of black people in the South during the time. *Black Boy* is at once an explanation and defense of Wright's separateness from a black community and a strong protest against the plight of all the black boys and girls, men and women subjected in his words, to "the ethics of living Jim Crow.". . .

RESISTING SOCIETY'S AUTHORITY

The relation which Wright establishes between his own personal experience and his generalized social views is clearly indicated (however unconsciously) in the famous passage occurring near the beginning of the second chapter where he bemoans what he sees as the shortcomings of black people which have come to be because of racism and segregation.

> After I had outlived the shocks of childhood, after the habit of reflection had been born in me, I used to mull over the strange absence of real kindness in Negroes, how unstable was our tenderness, how lacking in genuine passion we were, how void of great hope, how timid our joy, how bare our traditions, how hollow our memories, how lacking we were in those intangible sentiments that bind man to man, and how shallow was even our despair. . . . Whenever I thought of the essential bleakness of black life in America, I knew that Negroes had never been allowed to catch the full spirit of Western civilization, that they lived somehow in it but not of it.

If we look back to the conclusion of the first chapter, the coda which focuses on his father and his final alienation from him, we will find that the terms he uses to describe his father just a few paragraphs before are remarkably similar to the generalized observation about black people.

> From the white landowners to above him there had not been handed to him a chance to learn the meaning of loyalty, of sentiment, of tradition. Joy was as unknown to him as was despair. And a creature of the earth, he endured, hearty, whole, seemingly indestructible, with no regrets and no hope. He asked easy, drawling questions about me, his other son, his wife, and he laughed, amused, when I informed him of their destinies.

The fact that the generalized comment of the second chapter is parenthetical suggests that its relation to its context may be associational, that it does not necessarily follow strictly logically from what precedes it nor does it lead logically into what follows. The genesis of the unconscious associations of "father" and "orphans' home" is clear enough. His response to his escape from the home prompts the generalized comment which turns out then to be a judgment of his father, the implication being that it his father had caught the "full spirit of Western civilization," then he would not have been abandoned by him and would not ever have needed to be in the home.

The first chapter is, then, the autobiography's introduction. The remainder of the book fills in the details of the outline implied there, apprising us of the distance between Richard and everyone else in his environment. Even his brother is depicted as a shadowy figure, one who cannot be relied upon for support and protection from the untrustworthy children and adults, white and black, known and unknown, who people his world. Relatives, those who would ordinarily form the core of community, are enemies, at first potentially then actually so. Richard's relatives in their attempt to exert authority over him coerce, beat, or threaten him in a manner not entirely different from the way the white world menaces him if he does not give in to its demand that he submit to its authority. We learn finally that Wright resists the attempt of the white South to thrust identity and an alien sense of actuality on him by having learned to resist authority within the confines of his own family and community. Thus Richard Wright explains where he came from; how he got to be who he was at the time he wrote *Black Boy*.

Black Boy Is a Metaphor for the Birth of an Artist

Horace A. Porter

An assistant professor of English at Dartmouth College and contributor to numerous scholarly journals, Horace A. Porter contends that *Black Boy* and *American Hunger* are portraits of Wright as a developing young artist. Wright's struggle to master words, Porter says, parallels his struggle to become an individual and discover avenues of expression. In addition to providing Wright with the identity of writer, words help redeem him from the oppressive community that strives to stifle his imagination and help him fight against the prejudices of society at large.

As the curtain falls on the final page of *American Hunger*, the continuation of Richard Wright's autobiography, *Black Boy*, he is alone in his "narrow room, watching the sun sink slowly in the chilly May sky." Having just been attacked by former Communist associates as he attempted to march in the May Day parade, he ruminates about his life. He concludes that all he has, after living in both Mississippi and Chicago, are "words and a dim knowledge that my country has shown me no examples of how to live a human life." Wright ends his autobiography with the following words:

> I wanted to try to build a bridge of words between me and that world outside, that world which was so distant and elusive that it seemed unreal.

> I would hurl words into this darkness and wait for an echo, and if an echo sounded, no matter how faintly, I would send other words to tell, to march, to fight, to create a sense of the hunger for life that gnaws in us all, to keep alive in our hearts a sense of the inexpressibly human.

Excerpted from Horace A. Porter, "The Horror and the Glory: Richard Wright's Portrait of the Artist in *Black Boy* and *American Hunger*," in *Richard Wright: A Collection of Essays*, edited by Richard Macksey and Frank Moorer (Englewood Cliffs, NJ: Prentice Hall, 1984). Reprinted by permission of the author.

113

American Hunger (1977) is the continuation of *Black Boy* (1945). Wright initially composed them as one book entitled *The Horror and the Glory*. Thus, a reading of the two volumes as one continuous autobiography is crucial for a comprehensive understanding of his portrayal of himself as a young writer. Wright achieves remarkable poetic closure by bringing together at the end of *American Hunger* several interrelated themes which he elaborately spells out in *Black Boy*. The passage cited above illustrates his concern for words, his intense and troubling solitude, and his yearning to effect a revolution in the collective consciousness of America through the act of writing. In a sentence, the end of *American Hunger* is essentially the denouement of *Black Boy*.

Although critics have discussed the effect of Wright's early life on his writings, none has shown systematically how *Black Boy* (and to a lesser degree *American Hunger*) can be read primarily as a portrait of the artist as a young man. Consequently, I intend to demonstrate how the theme of words (with their transforming and redeeming power) is the nucleus around which ancillary themes swirl. Wright's incredible struggle to master words is inextricably bound to his defiant quest for individual existence and expression....

BANISHING THE FATHER

What one sees in Wright's autobiographies is how the behavior of his fanatically, religious grandmother, the painful legacy of his father, the chronic suffering of his mother, and how his interactions with blacks and whites both in and outside his immediate community are all thematically connected to the way Wright uses words to succeed as a writer and as a man.

The first chapter of *Black Boy*, the first scene, foreshadows the major theme—the development of the young artist's sensibility—of the book. Wright begins his narrative by recounting how he set fire to his house when he was four years old....

Wright may not have been completely aware of the psychological import of his opening scene. For, it appears that we must interpret young Wright's act of arson for what it really may have been. Perhaps even at that early age he was trying to free himself from the tyranny of his father's house in which his fanatically religious grandmother ruled: "I saw the image of my grandmother lying helplessly upon her bed and there were yellow flames in her black hair. . . ." The fact that young Wright has these thoughts while in "a dark hollow of a brick chimney . . . balled . . . into a tight knot," raises more profound psychological issues. Does this image represent a yearning to return to the womb? Does it constitute symbolic parricide? Does it symbolize the possibility of a new birth? When Wright sets his father's house aflame, he also makes an eloquent statement against the world the Southern slaveholders had made. Wright's later anxiety and guilt over having turned his back on his father's world drives him to write. His autobiography is an act of self-assertion and self-vindication in which he fearlessly confronts his father. Moreover, he demonstrates his love for his mother. And he pays homage to the anonymous, illiterate blacks whose world he fled.

In the process of moving away from his family and community, Wright began experiencing the problem (a consuming sense, of loss and abandonment) that was to become central to his life and his work. In certain primary respects, he was surely cognizant of the problem, but it operated on levels sufficiently profound as to be unfathomable later in his career. Numerous passages in *Black Boy* illustrate the phenomenon.

What has been characterized as ritual parricide comes readily to mind when Wright's father is awakened one day by the meowing of a stray cat his sons have found. Wright's father screams at him and his brother: "'Kill that damn thing!'" His father shouts, "'Do anything, but get it away from here!'" Ignoring the advice of his brother, Wright does exactly what his father suggests. He puts a rope around the cat's neck and hangs it. . . .

Note how Wright focuses on his father's words, how he attempts to neutralize his father's psychological authority by a willful misinterpretation of his statement.

At the end of the first chapter of *Black Boy*, Wright banishes his father from the remaining pages of both volumes of his autobiography. His father eventually deserts his mother and she struggles to support her two sons. On one occasion when Wright and his mother pay his father and his "strange woman" a visit in order to obtain money for food, Wright's father hands him a nickel. Wright refuses to accept the nickel, his father laughs and puts the nickel back in his pocket, stating, "'That's all I got.'" That image of his father was indelibly etched in Wright's memory. Wright states that over the years, his father's face would "surge up in my imagination so vivid and strong that I felt I could reach out and touch it; I would stare at it, feeling that it possessed some vital meaning which always eluded me."

Wright does not see his father for "a quarter of a century" after that encounter. His reunion with his father after a prolonged period leads to one of the more poignant and profound meditations of the autobiography. Staring at "the sharecropper, clad in ragged overalls, holding a muddy hoe in his gnarled, veined hands," Wright sees his biological father, but he also sees another man. The man standing before him is now both more and less than his father. . . .

Wright depicts his father as a "sharecropper," a "black peasant," whose actions and emotions are "chained . . . to the direct, animalistic impulses of his body." He and his father are "forever strangers, speaking a different language." Even in this passage which ostensibly has little to do with language, Wright reminds us that his ability to use and understand words has transformed him. His mind and consciousness have been "greatly and violently" altered. So Wright finally achieves the kind of authority he longed for as a kid. His father is no longer the threatening figure who told him to kill the kitten. From Wright's point of view, he has become something other; now, he is more phenomenon than person. Thus, Wright is simultaneously compassionate and dispassionate. On the one hand, he forgives his father; on the other, he clearly indicates that certain bonds between him and his father have been irreparably severed.

CONFLICTS OF THE MOTHER

Wright's mother also plays an important role in this psychological scheme of reconciliation and vindication. Despite the fact that his mother whipped him until he was unconscious after he set the house afire, he expresses tenderness toward her throughout *Black Boy*; Wright informs the reader that his mother was the first person who taught him to read and told him stories. After Wright had hanged the kitten in order to triumph over his father, he explains that his mother, who is "more imaginative, retaliated with an assault upon my sensibilities that crushed me with the moral horror involved in taking a life." His mother makes him bury the kitten that night and makes him pray.

Wright's mother not only instructs him in the high moral values of civilized society, but she also teaches him how to survive in a hostile and impoverished environment. She teaches him "the ethics of living Jim Crow." She frequently whips him because she knows that certain small gestures of self-pride and assertion would lead readily to brutality or death. Thus, if Wright's mother's arm is sometimes the arm of the oppressive social order, that same arm is, ironically, the tender, loving arm of the parent, nurturing and protecting her young. She instructs him in those traditions of black life that are sustaining—the necessity of learning to persevere, the ability to maintain grace under pressure, the practice of containing one's pain. Small wonder that Wright sees in his mother's suffering and in her will to live in spite of her rapidly declining health, a symbol of the numerous ills and injustices of the society in which they both live. . . .

Wright, the loving son, feels powerless before the seemingly vast impersonal forces which break his mother's spirit and ruin her health. His mother's life becomes a psychological and emotional charge to him; the "vital meaning" inherent in her suffering is the unstated psychological instruction to dedicate his life to the amelioration of the ills and injustices of society in whatever manner he finds appropriate and effective. Had Wright become indifferent toward the symbol of suffering his mother's life represents, his indifference would have been in effect psychological and moral betrayal of the first order. However, his reflections on his mother's suffering profoundly changes his whole attitude at the tender age of twelve. The spirit he catches sharpens the edges of his inchoate, artistic sensibility. We witness the writer's personality assuming self-conscious definition. . . .

Furthermore, the symbol of Wright's mother's suffering gives him hope. Long before he leaves the South he dreams of going North in order to "do something to redeem my being alive":

> I dreamed of going North and writing books, novels. The North symbolized to me all that I had not felt and seen; it had no relation whatever to what actually existed. Yet, by imagining a place where everything was possible, I kept hope alive in me. But where had I got this notion of doing something in the future, of going away from home and accomplishing something that would be recognized by others? I had, of course, read my Horatio Alger stories, and I knew my Get-Rich-Quick Wallingford series from cover to cover, though I

had sense enough not to hope to get rich . . . yet I felt I had to
go somewhere and do something to redeem my being alive.

Note that Wright considers the writing of books or novels as
the activity which would give his life meaning—"redeem my
being alive."

SALVATION IN WORDS

In the preceding pages, we discuss the subtle psychological
question of Wright's relationship to his parents. The task
now is to demonstrate specifically how Wright uses words to
remove himself from the oppressive community which tries
to stifle his imagination. Over the years, Wright becomes increasingly defiant and articulate. And the members of his
Southern community become suspicious of his goals and
motives.

Words lead to Wright's salvation and to his redemption.
From the first pages of *Black Boy*, the reader witnesses
Wright at the tender, impressionable age of six becoming a
messenger of the obscene. One day a black man drags
Wright, who is peering curiously through the doors of a saloon, inside. The unscrupulous and ignorant adults give him
liquor and send obscene messages by him back and forth to
one another. Wright goes from one person to the next shouting various obscenities in tune to the savage glee and laugh-
ter of the crowd. Surely, the incident makes Wright, inquisi-
tive as he is, wonder about the odd effects of his words.

He later learns his first lesson on the power of the written
word. Returning home after his first day of school during
which he had learned "all the four-letter words describing
physiological and sex functions," from a group of older boys,
he decides to display his newly acquired knowledge. Wright
goes from window to window in his neighborhood and
writes the words in huge soap letters. A woman stops him
and drives him home. That night the same woman informs
his mother of what Wright calls his "inspirational scrib-
blings." As punishment, she takes him out into the night
with a pail of water and a towel and demands that he erase
the words he had written: "'Now scrub until that word's
gone,' she ordered."

This comical incident may appears insignificant on the
surface. Furthermore, one cannot know the nature or the degree of the psychological effect the incident had on Wright.
However, it seems reasonable to assume that it had a signifi-

cant psychological impact. As Wright presents it, it is the first occasion on which words he writes are publicly censored; the first incident during which family members and neighbors become angry, if amused, because of words he writes. Wright states: "Neighbors gathered, giggling, muttering words of pity and astonishment, asking my mother how on earth I could have learned so much so quickly. I scrubbed at the four-letter soap words and grew blind with anger."

Wright's first written words are not the only words to get him in trouble. His first exposure to imaginative literature also causes a scene. One day a young school teacher, who boards with his grandmother, read to him *Bluebeard and His Seven Wives*. Wright describes the effect that the story has on him in visionary terms: "The tale made the world around me, throb, live. As she spoke reality changed, the look of things altered, and the world became peopled with magical presences. My sense of life deepened and the feel of things was different, somehow. Enchanted and enthralled. . . ."

Wright's visionary, enchanted state does not last. His grandmother screams "'you stop that you evil gal!'. . . 'I want none of that devil stuff in my house!'" When Wright insists that he likes the story and wants to hear what happened, his grandmother tells him, "'you're going to burn in hell. . . .'" Wright reacts strongly to this incident. He promises himself that when he is old enough, he "would buy all the novels there were and read them." Not knowing the end of the tale fills Wright with "a sense of emptiness and loss." He states that the tale struck "a profoundly responsive chord" in him. . . .

Given Wright's thirst for knowledge, his longing to achieve a self-conscious, independent manhood, his intense desire to live in a world elsewhere, he proves to be extremely vigilant in his fight against those, including his grandmother, his uncle, his aunt, and his high school principal, whom he calls his "tribal" oppressors. To Wright, theirs is at worst the path to poverty and ignorance, at best a path to what [Thomas] Mann's Tonio Kröger calls "the blisses of the commonplace." Wright wants neither.

Reflecting on his grandmother's insistence that he join the church and walk in the path of righteousness (as she sees it), Wright states: "We young men had been trapped by the community, the tribe in which we lived and which we were a part. The tribe for its own safety was asking us to be at one with it. . . . Moreover, commenting on how the community views anyone who chooses not to have his soul saved, Wright asserts:

> This business of saving souls had no ethics; every human relationship was shamelessly exploited. In essence, the tribe was asking us whether we shared its feeling; if we refused to join the church, it was equivalent to saying no, to placing ourselves in the position of moral monsters.

It is important to keep in mind that Wright's mother is an exception. To be sure, she shares many of the views of the community, but out of love, she aids Wright in his attempt to escape the tribe. Speaking of his mother after the Bluebeard incident, Wright says: "I burned to learn to read novels and I tortured my mother into telling me the meaning of every strange word I saw, not because the word itself had any value, but because it was the gateway to a forbidden and enchanting land."

Against the wishes of the community, Wright continues to read and develop as a young writer. His first real triumph comes when the editor of the local Negro newspaper accepts one of Wright's stories, "The Voodoo of Hell's Half-Acre." The plot of the story involves a villain who wants a widow's home. After the story is published, no one, excepting the newspaper editor, gives any encouragement. His grandmother calls it "'the devil's work'"; his high school principal objects to his use of "hell" in the story's title; even his mother feels that his writing will make, people feel that he is "weak minded." His classmates do not believe that he has written the story. . . .

THE OUTSIDER

Herein, Wright identifies another problem which menaces him throughout his writing life. The problem is the young artist's radical disassociation of sensibility from that of the group. In this regard, he is reminiscent of the young artist heroes of Thomas Mann and James Joyce, of Tonio Kröger and Stephen Daedalus. However, Wright's plight as a young artist is significantly different in a crucial way. His is not simply the inability to experience, by dint of his poetic sensibility, "the blisses of the commonplace." Not only is Wright pitted against his immediate family and community, the tribe, as he calls them. He must also fight against the prejudices of the larger society.

Wright wrote "The Voodoo of Hell's Half-Acre" when he was fifteen. He concludes:

> Had I been conscious of the full extent to which I was push-
> ing against the current of my environment, I would have been
> frightened altogether out of my attempts at writing. . . .

> I was building up in me a dream which the entire educational
> system of the South had been rigged to stifle. I was feeling the
> very thing that the state of Mississippi had spent millions of
> dollars to make sure that I would never feel; I was becoming
> aware of the thing that the Jim Crow laws had been drafted
> and passed to keep out of my consciousness; I was acting on
> impulses that Southern senators in the nation's capital had
> striven to keep out of Negro life. . . .

A telling example which brilliantly demonstrates what
Wright means in the passage cited above involves his love
for words and books once again. When Wright is nineteen,
he reads an editorial in the Memphis *Commercial Appeal*
which calls H. L. Mencken a fool. Wright knows that
Mencken is the editor of the *American Mercury* and he wonders what Mencken has done to deserve such scorn. . . .

His reading of Mencken provides him with a formidable
reading list: Anatole France, Joseph Conrad, Sinclair Lewis,
Sherwood Anderson, Dostoyevski, George Moore, Flaubert,
Maupassant, Tolstoy, Frank Harris, Twain, Hardy, Crane,
Zola, Norris, Gorky, Bergson, Ibsen, Shaw, Dumas, Poe,
Mann, Dreiser, Eliot, Gide, Stendhal, and others. Wright
starts reading many of the writers Mencken mentions.
Moreover, the general effect of his reading was to make him
more obsessive about it: "Reading grew into a pas-
sion. . . . Reading was like a drug, a dope."

Mencken provides Wright with far more than a convenient reading list of some of the greater masters. He becomes an "example to Wright—perhaps an idol—both in
matters of style and vocational perspective or stance. . . .

A NEW BEGINNING

A few months after reading Mencken, Wright finds the convenient opportunity to flee to the North. He closes *Black Boy*
on an optimistic note.

American Hunger opens with Wright's arrival in Chicago
and with the din of that windy city entering his consciousness, mocking his treasured fantasies. Wright had envi-
sioned Chicago as a city of refuge. However, his first years
are "long years of semi-starvation." He works as a dish-

washer, part-time post office clerk, life insurance salesman, and laboratory custodian. Since none of these jobs lasts long, finding adequate food and shelter becomes extremely difficult. At one point, Wright shares a windowless rear room with his mother and younger brother. But good luck occasionally comes in the guise of ill. Many of the experiences he has while working odd jobs supplies revelations which subsequently form the core of his best fiction. Wright probably would not have written *Native Son* if he had not seen and felt Bigger Thomas's rage.

The first half of *American Hunger* is primarily devoted to a sociopsychological portrayal of Wright's life and work among the black and white poor. Wright shows how ignorance and racial discrimination fuel prejudice and self-hatred. He gives us glimpses of *les miserables,* who are corrupted, exploited, and destroyed. While working as an insurance salesman, Wright himself aids in the swindling of the black poor. Yet we are aware throughout that his is a form of predatory desperation. His is the hard choice between honesty and starvation.

Communists dominate the second half of *American Hunger.* As Wright tells his story, he has strong reservations about the party from the outset and gets involved indirectly. He becomes a member of the party primarily because he is a writer and he leaves it for the same reason. Lacking intellectual communion and meaningful social contacts, he joins Chicago's John Reed Club. The members enthusiastically welcome him, and he is immediately given a writing assignment for *Left Front.* After only two months and due to internal rivalry, Wright is elected Executive Secretary of the club. He humbly declines the nomination at first, but, after some insistent prodding, reluctantly accepts the position. Thus, though not a Communist, he heads one of the party's leading cultural organizations. Given his independence of mind, however, he raises too many troubling questions for party officials and they soon begin to wage a war against him. They try to harness his imagination and whip it down the official ideological path. But Wright is already at work on the stories of his first book, *Uncle Tom's Children.* He writes: "Must I discard my plot ideas and seek new ones? No. I could not. My writing was my way of seeing, my way of living, my way of feeling, and who could change his sight, his notion of direction, his senses?"

Wright dwells rather tediously on the Communist party in the six brief chapters of *American Hunger.* However, he does devote limited space to the story of how he "managed to keep humanly alive through transfusions from books" and the story of how he learned his craft: "working nights I spent my days in experimental writing, filling endless pages with stream-of-consciousness Negro dialect, trying to depict the dwellers of the Black Belt as I felt and saw them." And ever conscious of the need to refine his craft, Wright moved into other realms. He read Stein's *Three Lives,* Crane's *The Red Badge of Courage,* and Dostoyevski's *The Possessed.* He strove to achieve the "dazzling magic" of Proust's prose in *A Remembrance of Things Past:* "I spent hours and days pounding out disconnected sentences for the sheer love of words. . . . I strove to master words, to make them disappear, to make them important by making them new, to make them melt into a rising spiral of emotional stimuli, each feeding and reinforcing the other, and all ending in an emotional climax that would drench the reader with a sense of a new world. That was the single aim of my living."

Finally Wright was able to redeem himself with words. They moved him from Mississippi to Chicago to New York and eventually made Paris his home town. Using words, he hurled himself at the boundary lines of his existence. Goethe's saying that "Man can find no better retreat from the world than art, and man can find no stronger link with the world than art" sums up the conundrum of Wright's life.

The Theme of Education in *Black Boy*

William A. Proefriedt

William A. Proefriedt is professor of philosophy of education and American studies at Queens College, City University of New York. Here, he describes how Richard Wright gained a broad, informal education as an outsider moving among a variety of communities, both as a child and as an adult. Proefriedt maintains that Wright felt the ambiguity of wanting to belong to a community and yet remain alone. He builds barriers and distances himself from others throughout his life and rebels against formal education and white America's definition of his roles as a young black man in the South.

A great deal of thinking about educating people who move from one culture to another has gone on in this country in the twentieth century. At its best, this thinking has focused on the ways in which equality of opportunity could be enhanced for an immigrant population through educational means. At its very best, questions of cultural identity, and a concern with the value of the native culture of immigrants, have been included. At its worst, concerns with order and with a careless assimilation have occupied center stage.

In all of this, those moving from one culture to another have been viewed as presenting an educational problem. There surely are senses in which that is the case. But it is also the case that for some persons the experience of moving between or among cultures is undergone in ways that are profoundly educational. Further, an analysis of the educational dimensions of this experience raises questions about our understanding of educational purposes. I will argue that the immigrant experience serves as metaphor for what it means to be genuinely educated in the modern world.

Excerpted from William A. Proefriedt, "The Immigrant or 'Outsider' Experience as Metaphor for Becoming an Educated Person in the Modern World: Mary Antin, Richard Wright, and Eva Hoffman," *Melus,* vol. 16, no. 2 (Summer 1989/1990). Reprinted with permission from the publisher. (Notes in the original have been omitted in this reprint.)

I base my argument on reading that I have been doing recently in the autobiographies of immigrants and other outsiders. I began these studies with an interest in looking at passages in the autobiographies that referred specifically to schooling experience, but I soon realized that however important a role schooling played in these works, the most significant educational phenomena were taking place in the ways in which individuals constructed their experience of movement between and among cultures. . . .

Richard Wright . . . grew up in a situation in which he was alienated from his peers, his family, the religious community to which family members belonged, and most of all from the white society of the American South of the early part of this century. More than a third of the way through his autobiography, filled with details of his extraordinary and conflict-filled childhood, Wright reports that he was enrolled in a Seventh-Day Adventist School in which his Aunt Addie taught. He describes his fellow students as docile, without will, and emotionally flat.

> I was able to see them with an objectivity that was inconceivable to them. They were claimed wholly by their environment and could imagine no other, whereas I had come from another plane of living from the swinging doors of saloons, the railroad yard, the roundhouses, the street gangs, the river levees, an orphan home; had shifted from town to town and home to home; had mingled with grownups more than perhaps was good for me.

Wright here turns what might have been a summary lament for the displacement and the wide and cruel experiences of his childhood into a celebration of the broadened capacities his moving among multiple societies had engendered in him and a recognition that the other boys in the school had suffered a narrowing of their perceptual and imaginative possibilities in the univocal environments in which they had grown.

Wright . . . feels the ambiguity of desiring to be a part of a community and of relishing his aloneness. He moves to a public school, and in a grocery store at lunchtime with his classmates, he goes hungry rather than tell them that his grandmother has, for religious reasons, forbidden him to work on Saturdays, and that, consequently, he has no money:

> Again and again I vowed that some day I would end this hunger of mine, this apartness, this eternal difference; and I

did not suspect that I would never get intimately into their lives, that I was doomed to live with them but not of them, that I had my own strange and separate road, a road which in later years would make them wonder how I came to tread it.

Later, Wright and his mother joined a Methodist church. He longed also to be a part of this community, but he remained the observer. "I liked it and I did not like it: I longed to be among them, yet when with them I looked at them as if I were a million miles away." He liked the people in the church, and they urged him to become a member, to be baptized. At a revival meeting, he tells us, the preacher separated the few non-church members from the others. The mothers of these boys and other church members prayed and sang hymns while they awaited the boys' decisions to come forward and be baptized.

> The mothers knelt. My mother grabbed my hands and I felt hot tears scalding my fingers. I tried to stifle my disgust. We young men had been trapped by the community, the tribe in which we lived and of which we were a part. The tribe, for its own safety, was asking us to be at one with it.

Wright tells us that if he refused to join the church, which was equated with refusing to love his mother, he would be perceived as a moral monster. His mother pulled his arm and he walked with her to the preacher. "I had not felt anything except sullen anger and a crushing sense of shame. Yet I was somehow glad that I had got it over with; no barriers now stood between me and the community." But, of course, Wright would rebuild the barriers, and re-enact the drama of joining, distancing himself from, evaluating, and leaving other communities throughout his life.

AN EDUCATION IN RACISM

Whatever conflicts Wright had with family, friends, and church paled beside his collision with the culture of the white South. His mother was at first unwilling to explain to him just how matters stood between white and black society in the early decades of the twentieth century. But he soon became aware of the dangerous situation in which he lived. He heard a story of a black woman whose husband had been killed by a white mob. She asked to recover her husband's body, and with a weapon concealed in the sheets in which she was to wrap the body, she shot four of his killers. This story captured the imagination of Wright, who felt powerless in his dealing with older whites, and he fantasized about repeating the woman's actions if he were faced with a white mob.

Throughout his life, Wright refused to behave in ways others expected; this was especially true in his relations with whites. He celebrated this confrontational quality in himself and saw it as crucial to the person and writer he was to become. Just as he rebelled against the formal public educational system, he rebelled also against the values and practices which constituted the informal education system for Blacks in the American South. He refused to accept white definitions of what it meant to be a young black man, prompting one of his classmates, advising him about getting a job, to warn him to learn how to live in the South if he didn't want to get killed. "'Dick,' his friend, Griggs, warned him, 'look, you're black, black, black. Can't you understand that?'" It is this sort of learning, this sort of understanding that most of us being inducted into communities are quite good at. We learn our roles, playing them out in an unquestioning fashion. We remain unaware of other options. We perform the roles defined for us by a community in order to be fully accepted into it. But Wright, who was alienated from family members, from his closest friends, and from his religious community, who had refused to accept his place in communities which arguably had much to offer him was not about to pay the price in belief, attitude and behavior to gain acceptance by southern whites.

His friend urged him to think before he acted or spoke.

> What Griggs was saying was true, but it was simply utterly impossible for me to calculate, to scheme, to act, to plot all the time. I would remember to dissemble for short periods, then I would forget and act straight and human again, not with the desire to harm anybody, but merely forgetting the artificial status of race and class.

This forgetting on Wright's part does not, of course, represent a flight from consciousness of his situation, but a refusal to go down a road in which behaviors that begin as dissimulation end as defining the self. He contrasts his inability to learn his role with the abilities of his peers who learn theirs all too well. Speaking of young black men working with him as hotel employees when he was seventeen, Wright says,

> I began to marvel at how smoothly the black boys acted out the roles that the white race had mapped out for them. Most of them were not conscious of living a special separate,

stunted way of life. Yet I knew that in some period of their growing up—a period that they had no doubt forgotten—there had been developed in them a delicate sensitive controlling mechanism that shut off their minds and emotions from all that the white race had said was taboo.

STEPPING OUTSIDE THE LAWS FOR BLACKS AND WHITES

Here is the real loss of consciousness, the real forgetting that allows a kind of learning, a learning of roles imposed by those with no intention of allowing the young black men full participation in the larger community. Wright understood the nature of the social pedagogy at work, saw the tragedy of the internalization of white values by those who "learned" what it was to be black.

Wright's understanding of the ways in which he was perceived by whites in power left him feeling lost. He never knew when he would make a mistake and be punished for it. He sensed the arbitrariness of this world in relation to him. "I no longer felt bound by the laws which white and black were supposed to obey in common. I was outside these laws; the white people had told me so." Wright perceived the deception and despotism at the heart of the laws and institutions of the white society, and its cynical purposes in assigning demeaning roles to blacks. And so he stepped outside.

It is easy to read Wright's autobiography as only a rejection of his childhood and the people and places that were a part of it. He tells us,

> I was building up in me a dream which the entire educational system of the South had been rigged to stifle. I was feeling the very thing that the state of Mississippi had spent millions of dollars to make sure that I would never feel. . . . In me was shaping a yearning for a kind of consciousness, a mode of being that the way of life about me had said could not be, must not be, and upon which the penalty of death had been placed.

. . . A full understanding of Wright must capture both the rejection and the celebration of childhood and identify precisely what is being rejected and what is being celebrated.

At two separate points in his autobiography, Wright pauses in the naturalistic descriptions of the terrors of his childhood, to offer in a lyrical, incantatory style, impressions of the sights and sounds of his childhood.

> There was the delight I caught in seeing long, straight rows of red and green vegetables stretching away in the sun to the bright horizon.

> There was the faint cool kiss of sensuality when drew came
> on to my cheeks and shins as I ran down the wet garden
> paths in the early morning.

> There was the vague sense of the infinite, as I looked down
> upon the yellow, dreaming waters of the Mississippi River
> from the verdant bluffs of Natchez.

These powerful and positive memories of his childhood
surely were the beginnings of the intense and energetic experiencing of the world that Wright was to carry with him
throughout his life. At his grandmother's home in Jackson, a
young boarder, a schoolteacher named Ella, tells a still very
young Richard the story of Bluebeard. "The tale made the
world around me be, throb, live. As she spoke, reality
changed, the look of things altered and the world became
peopled with magical presences." Wright's lively experience
of the world was enhanced by stories, and though he was
forbidden to read fiction, he eventually began writing it himself, taking an odd pleasure in the fact that his earliest readers were baffled by his imaginative efforts. Wright tells us
that by the time he was twelve he had already developed an
attitude toward life that he would carry with him. He saw
himself as skeptical, seeking, tolerant yet critical, sympathetic, and at once tender and cruel, violent and peaceful.

He looked for the suffering in others he knew he would
find. ". . . It [the attitude he had developed as a child] made
me love talk that sought answers to questions that could help
nobody, that could only keep alive in me the enthralling
sense of wonder and awe in the face of the drama of human
feeling which is hidden by the external drama of life."
Wright himself then tells us that his fundamental emotional
and intellectual attitudes toward life were formulated in his
childhood in Mississippi. That these experiences are reported as cruel and terrifying ones does not undermine his
claim; they were nevertheless transformed by him into educational experiences, experiences that helped to form the in-
quiring and sympathetic attitude toward the world he describes.

But Wright did leave things behind him, rejected them,
moved into a genuinely new life. There were real tensions
and ambiguities when he looked back on that old life
through the eyes of a man who had taken as his own American and World literature, who had gone to Chicago and New
York, who had lived an active political, personal, and literary

life, and who was about to take his place on the world stage. He speaks of coming back to see his father, a quarter-century after they had been separated. He sees the two of them as for-ever strangers. "I was overwhelmed to realize that he could never understand me or the scalding experiences that had swept me beyond his life and into an area of living that he could never know." The early fear of his father had turned to a distancing. There was a gulf. New things had been learned. There was also understanding from a new perspective, a looking at the past through a new conceptual structure. With Wright . . . there was an educationally fruitful ambiguity, a painful double vision of the world.

The Metaphor of the Journey in *Black Boy*

Robert J. Butler

A professor of English at Canisius College in Buffalo, New York, Robert J. Butler discusses the drive for movement in American culture and the theme of movement in *Black Boy* in particular. Change of place is intrinsically valuable to Wright, he says, as it endows his life with a sense of energy and purpose. While Wright's "outer journeys" often end in paralysis, his inner voyage, centered around the development of his consciousness, allows him freedom to move in productive ways.

One of the central drives in American culture is a quest for pure motion, movement either for its own sake or as a means of freeing oneself from a prior mode of existence. A relatively new and chronically rootless society, America has always set an unusually high premium on mobility rather than stability. It is not surprising, therefore, that American literature is densely populated with heroes who try as Tennessee Williams says, "to find in motion what was lost in space," fundamentally restless people in search of settings which are fluid enough to accommodate their passion for radical forms of freedom and independence. . . .

Although American and Afro-American literary traditions are quite different in many important ways, they are in essential agreement on this way of imagining movement. The journey motif, which is central to both traditions, is often aggressively non-teleological; that is, it nearly always resists being directed toward a particular place and instead exults in movement through indefinite space. Unlike representative journey books from English and European traditions, American and Afro-American classics are typically open-ended in nature. They view movement and change as in-

Excerpted from Robert J. Butler, "The Quest for Pure Motion in Richard Wright's *Black Boy*," *Melus*, vol. 10, no. 3 (Fall 1983). Reprinted with permission from the publisher. (Notes and/or references in the original have been omitted in this reprint.)

trinsically valuable—a process of becoming rather than progress culminating in a state of completed being. As such these journeys are a compelling metaphor of the American desire for the "new life" consisting of unlimited personal development. . . .

POSSIBILITY THROUGH MOVEMENT

Richard Wright is noted for his trapped heroes, especially figures such as Bigger Thomas, Fred Daniels, and Cross Damon, but he has also written powerfully of the quest for open motion. Both "The Man Who Was Almos' a Man" and "Big Boy Leaves Home" end with bittersweet images of the heroes moving vaguely North in search of new lives which may or may not be available to them. *The Long Journey* concludes with its central character on "a journey that would take him far, far away" from a restrictive past toward new possibilities. These narratives evoke simultaneously allusions to the journey across the River Jordan celebrated by the spirituals, the odyssey down the road extolled by the blues, and the search for open space which resonates through our classic literature. All of these works, to use Walt Whitman's phrase, "tramp a perpetual journey" toward varying degrees of freedom and independence.

Although Wright is often described as a natural genius who wrote about raw experiences unfiltered through any literary traditions, he was, as Michel Fabre has cogently argued, a very well-read man who was acutely aware of the "dual heritage of the Black writer in America." *Black Boy*, which is essentially structured as a search for an open journey, drinks thirstily from the deep streams of Black folk literature and American picaresque literature. As a result, it portrays Wright's own life as very different from Bigger Thomas' trapped existence. Although he had to struggle hard against the racist environment which paralyzed many of his characters, Wright was able to liberate himself and thus give free play to what Ellison has called his "almost manic restlessness." Far from being a sign of purposelessness and incoherence, Wright's pursuit of open motion endowed his life with real energy and purpose. Indeed, it helps to account for his triumph as a man and an artist.

In its most basic terms, *Black Boy* presents a world with two basic options: 1) human suffocation which is dramatized with images of stasis, and 2) human possibility which is rendered by images of constant movement. To emphasize this polarity, Wright repeatedly contrasts scenes of motion and stasis throughout the book. For example, the terrifying opening scene of entrapment is artfully counterpointed with the Whitmanesque prose poem which immediately follows it. Unlike *Native Son*, which is telescoped by the opening scene of paralysis, *Black Boy* begins with two scenes which define the book's central drives.

Confined in a house with a bed-ridden grandmother, Wright as a four-year-old boy looks "yearningly" out into the empty street, all the while "dreaming of running and playing and shouting." From the beginning, his protean imagination is set in opposition to a flat, enervated environment which denies his impulses any creative outlet. Wandering "listlessly" about the room, he can find nothing interesting except the "shimmering embers" and "quivering coals" of the fire. Even after he has been cautioned by his mother not to play with the fire, he feels irresistibly drawn to this fluid medium and soon sets the curtains ablaze. Although his immediate reaction is "to run away and never come back," he merely hides under the house which he falsely regards as "a place of safety." He breaks into "a wild run" when his father pulls him out of the crawl space but is easily caught and then severely beaten by his mother, to the extent that he is bed-ridden for five days. This scene ends on a note of painful ambivalence with Wright "determined to run away" but "lost in a fog of fear." As Michel Fabre has observed, this episode left lasting scars on Wright, shattering his emotional security and initiating an "estrangement" which deepened as Wright grew older. Indeed, the "red circles" of flame which consume the curtains, can be seen as a revealing symbol of Wright's early life—a trap of spreading violence which can easily destroy him if the fails to understand and find alternatives to it.

In addition, the prose poem which immediately follows this scene, gives some clues about what these alternatives might be. Here Wright is outdoors, moving in a world of imaginative, physical, and emotional freedom. Whereas in the previous scene his consciousness was blocked by fear, he now relaxes and expands his sensibilities, as experience reveals its "coded meanings" to him. Significantly, the poem is suffused with lyrical images of indefinite motion: horses clopping down a dusty road; Wright himself running

through wet garden paths in the early morning; the Mississippi River winding past the bluffs of Natchez; wild geese
flying South for the winter; a solitary ant moving on "a mysterious journey"; and "vast hazes of gold" which "washed
earthward from star-heavy skies on silent nights." The implications of this startling juxtaposition of scenes are clear.
Even in the harshly restrictive world of segregated Mississippi there are avenues of escape and development. Once
liberated from society, which in *Black Boy* is always a trap,
Wright can discover a protean world offering human possibilities.

As is the case in much American writing, the physical liberation literally described by the poem almost always generates emotional and spiritual freedom. Although the net effect of the opening scene is to bottle up Wright's feelings,
here he feels wonder at the horses, nostalgia for the geese,
and languor from the rustling leaves. These images also
spring meanings which have significant spiritual overtones.
The waters of the Mississippi evoke "a sense of the infinite,"
the movements of the lone ant are described as "mysterious," and the motion of the stars instills in him a deep religious awe. In short, motion endows life with vitality and
meaning, transforming a dead world of routine into a dynamic realm of beauty where the self can be transformed.

ON MOTION OR STASIS

Wright carefully develops this contrast between motion and
stasis throughout *Black Boy*. The Memphis tenement in
which he lives as a young man is set in opposition to the
steamboat ride on the Mississippi which fires his imagination. The terror he initially feels at being locked out of his
house is dissolved into fascination by his "irresistible" impulse to roam the streets of the city. The scene where he
again hides under his bed to avoid a beating from his grandmother is likewise contrasted with a second prose poem
filled with images of movement—chasing butterflies, observing the "rolling sweep of tall green grass," and enjoying
"nights of drizzling rain." The closed world of Mississippi is
always sharply differentiated from the open world of his developing spirit.

Black Boy, therefore, has a narrative structure which is
complexly double, giving us two opposite but thematically
related plot patterns. Wright's outer journey takes the form

of a series of apparently random moves which end in paralysis. In contrast to this naturalistic fable, strongly resembling the plots of works such as *Maggie: A Girl of the Streets* and *McTeague*, is an inward narrative which is centered around the development of the hero's consciousness which will enable him eventually to move in freer, more productive ways. As such, it is a story of awakening and is closely related to Dreiser's *Dawn* and Farrell's autobiographical novels about Danny O'Neill.

An even cursory examination of the outer narrative of *Black Boy* vividly demonstrates that Wright's physical movements during his early life were a bewildering road leading nowhere. As Keneth Kinnamon has revealed, Wright lived in no less than nineteen residences in his first nineteen years. The result of this incoherent movement from one racist place to another was to strip Wright of both familial bonds and a meaningful self image, thus depriving him of any emotional center to his life. The results of such a life of perpetual drifting are clear to Wright as he observes the people around him. His father's life is an especially painful object lesson, for he sees it as environmentally-controlled movement leading to eventual depletion:

> I stood before him, poised, my mind aching as it embraced the simple nakedness of his life, feeling how completely his soul was *imprisoned* by the slow flow of the seasons, by wind and rain and sun, how *fastened* were his memories to a crude and raw past, how *chained* were his actions and emotions to the direct, animalistic impulses of his withering body.

Since nothing directs the father's life but the restrictive motions of nature, his movements eventually wind down to a terrifying stasis. After deserting the family and wandering restlessly around the North where he becomes "hopelessly snarled" in the city, he returns to the South to live out his days in a form of slavery, sharecropping. His life then is very much like the flame described in Chapter One, a circle of necessity which consumes him.

Wright's view of his grandmother and mother are also portrayed with images of futility. Unlike his father who was associated with blind movement, the grandmother is always described in terms of an equally disastrous inertia. Initially presented as immobilized in a sick bed, she is throughout the novel mentally and spiritually imprisoned by an absolute commitment to a fundamentalist religion which separates her from anything vital in life. Her house in Jackson provides a kind of locus for Wright since it is the place to which he keeps returning after his various moves, but it is always a dead center of repression and he usually feels a sense of claustrophobia there. His deepest wish is simply to run away from such a "home" as soon as he grows old enough to do so.

An even more important image of futility is provided by his mother, whose suffering becomes a tragic epiphany of the wasted life. After a stroke leaves her partially paralyzed, she is often seen in bed or, like Dreiser's Hurstwood, rocking in a chair while gazing blankly into oblivion. Indeed, one of the central passages in *Black Boy* is Wright's agonized meditation on his mother's condition:

> That night I ceased to react to my mother; my feelings were frozen. . . . Her illness gradually became an accepted thing in the house, something that could not be stopped or helped.
>
> My mother's suffering grew into a symbol in my mind, gathering to itself all the poverty, the ignorance, the helplessness, the painful, baffling, hunger-ridden hours, the restless moving, the futile seeking, the uncertainty, the fear, the dread, the meaningless pain and endless suffering. Her life set an emotional tone for my life.

The forms of moral and physical paralysis characterizing the lives of his parents and grandmother become for Wright an index of the roles assigned to Blacks in Southern society, all of which result in "meaningless suffering."

It is his task to "wring a meaning" out of such suffering. Although he eventually comes to see the South as a Dantean hell where he is "forever condemned, ringed by walls," he nevertheless is able to achieve salvation of sorts by moving along his "own strange and separate road." Caught in a society which is intent on reducing his life to random drifting, disintegration, and paralysis, he is able to find a meaningful alternative in his own inwardness: "Because I had no power to make things happen outside me, I made things happen within me." Crucial to this purposeful inward narrative is Wright's gradual mastery of language through reading and writing, a process which is always associated with images of motion and release. Even the cheap pulp thrillers he reads as a boy become "a gateway to the world" because they transport him from the locked room in which he reads to "outlandish men in faraway, outlandish cities." Energizing his imagination, they provide Wright access to an open world.

Ella, the boarder at his grandmother's house, can feed his starved imagination on the literature which serves as an alternative to his grandmother's mind-numbing religiosity:

> As her words fell upon my ears I endowed them with a reality that *welled up* somewhere within me. . . . The tale made the world around me be, *throb*, live. As she spoke, *reality changed*, the look of things altered, and the world became peopled with magical presences. My sense of life deepened. . . . My imagination *blazed*.

This rich proliferation of motion images, which portrays his mind bubbling, the world throbbing and his imagination blazing, suggests that his active use of language has dissolved the harshly fixed limits of Southern life. Restrictive place has been turned into open space—a universe of growth.

AN INWARD JOURNEY

The stages of Wright's inward journey can be clearly measured by what he reads and writes. His first story, a crude potboiler entitled *The Voodoo of Hell's Half Acre*, pushes him "against the current of his environment" because it flaunts his distaste for the conventional expectations imposed upon him. And he gets a sense of the free movements possible in American life by eagerly devouring Horatio Alger novels and westerns such as Zane Grey's *Riders of the Purple Sage*. When his reading of H.L. Mencken's *A Book of Prefaces* introduces him to serious modern writers such as Theodore Dreiser, Sinclair Lewis, Emile Zola, and Hart Crane, he moves forward in great leaps. Books by these writers serve as "vicarious cultural transfusions" which give him "new ways of looking and seeing." They unlock the doors of his consciousness, thus opening up his inner and outer universe. Armed now with an awareness that gives him a much-needed "sense of distance between [himself] and the world in which [he] lived," he can progress to liberating new worlds.

His journey North, therefore, should be viewed as quite different from his father's failed attempts to leave the South. Whereas his father's actions amounted to simple desertion and evasion, Wright left the South so that he could more fully engage himself with reality:

> I fled so that the numbness of my defensive living might thaw out and let me feel the pain . . . of what living in the South had meant.

His father's travels resulted in his being hopelessly "snarled in the city," but Northern urban life, for all of its harshness, sends Wright on an open journey "toward alien and undreamed-of shores of knowing." Because they have lived on such "vastly different planes of reality," Wright is able to transcend the geographical and social "places" which blighted his father's life.

Like Huck Finn, who also becomes something radically different from his father, Wright cuts himself loose from the very idea of place and defines himself ultimately in terms of free space. By the end of *Black Boy* he has a firm and clear awareness that all of the places which he has experienced have threatened to cripple his spirit. The orphanage in Memphis, the Grandmother's house in Jackson, his Uncle Clark's house in Greenwood, and the rented rooms he and his mother retreat to in Arkansas are all prisons of one kind or another. And the various social positions offered to him along the way are even worse traps. All of the jobs he has held are ways of fixing him in a rigidly defined "place" in Southern society. Similarly, the apparently liberating role of teacher extended to him by his school principal is only a way of selling out. Even Miss Moss, the woman in Memphis who sincerely offers him her daughter and her home, must be rejected, for he knows that she will put a "hold" on his spirit. Instinctively and consciously recoiling against all of these notions of place, Wright sets himself in open motion in pursuit of a protean self which, as Whitman has declared, is too large to be realized in one location. For American identity, which is premised upon continual metamorphosis, can only be realized by moving through a world of endless flux.

Phyllis Rauch Klotman has argued that the apparently hopeful ending of *Black Boy* is really undercut by the fact that the narrative concludes before Wright can describe the disturbing experiences in Chicago which eventually were published separately in *American Hunger*. Knowing what we know of Wright's disappointments in Chicago and recognizing the stark treatment which that city received in *Native Son*, she concludes: "The promise of the North is a delusion, of course; it is the walled confines of Bigger Thomas' existence in Chicago."

But this is misleading in two ways. First, it fails to distinguish between Bigger's failed journey, which is traced to his tragically limited consciousness, and Wright's odyssey which was the result of his hard-won awareness of himself and his world. Whereas Bigger sees Chicago as a dark labyrinth which frustrates his desires for movement and de-velopment, Wright himself had a much more balanced and complicated vision of Chicago. It was for him both a night-mare world suggestive of Poe and the sort of rough open uni-verse celebrated by Dreiser and Sandburg, a city of wonder and terror. As he points out in "How Bigger Was Born," Chicago is a "fabulous . . . indescribable city" of dramatic "extremes." It was at once a world of "high idealism and hard cynicism," a young city fresh from "the windswept prairies," but also an ancient city replete with images of "man's age-old destiny." In its raw vitality and cosmopolitan diversity, it was a vastly better environment for Wright than the fetid cage he had left in Mississippi. Never idealized, it nonetheless provided him with a symbol of American iden-tity, the larger world for which he hungered.

But Klotman's interpretation of the ending of *Black Boy* is defective on more serious grounds. In claiming that Wright's journey North was undercut by his actual experiences in Chicago, she implies that Chicago as a specific place was the end point of his flight. As this paper has tried to demonstrate, Wright did not leave Memphis for Chicago; he left the South for the North. The North for Wright was more a state of mind and a human ideal than a fully reified location, for it "sym-bolized to [him] all that [he] had not felt and seen; it had no relation to what actually existed." It is, as Robert Stepto has recently observed, "a symbolic space" keeping the hero imaginatively and morally alive. In this sense, it is altogether appropriate that *Black Boy* is "cut off" with the train ride out of Memphis as Wright contemplates the rich image of the ever-moving stars.

EMBRACING THE DYNAMIC UNIVERSE

Black Boy, therefore, concludes with an image that naturally calls forth a marvelous range of literary associations sug-gesting Dante's *Commedia*, the spirituals, and Fitzgerald's *The Great Gatsby*. Like Dante, Wright was not searching for a particular social world so much as some "redeeming meaning" to life. The stars to which he aspires are also like the North Star so powerfully rendered in the spirituals—di-rections pointing to general areas of freedom rather than any one spot. And the book's ultimate image also evokes Gatsby's endless climb up the ladder to the stars, a source of possibility and wonder. . . . Western, American, and Afro-American traditions thus resonate at the end of *Black Boy* in a deep and complex harmony, producing a work of great richness, a landmark in modern autobiography.

Although most critics have argued that Wright's alienation from a stable social world was simply traumatic for him, the fact is that he was able to overcome the shock of alienation necessitated by circumstances, translating it into an affirmative picaresque vision. Wright, who never really stopped moving after he left the South, could later observe:

> I'm a rootless man but I'm neither psychologically distraught nor in any wise particularly perturbed because of it. Personally I do not hanker after, and seem not to need, as many emotional attachments, sustaining roots, or idealistic allegiances as most people. I declare unabashedly that I like and even cherish the state of abandonment, of aloneness; it does not bother me; indeed it seems the natural, inevitable condition of man, and I welcome it. I can make a home almost anywhere on this earth.

The fact that *Black Boy* concludes with a journey centered around a hero with "hazy notions" and "devoid of any real sense of direction" does not undercut the affirmative meaning of such a journey. Rather, it indicates that the hero has achieved a spirit as protean as the world he finally enters. At last freed from the segregated society which had earlier "trapped" him, and also liberated from his own deep-seated fears, he can now become an artist who embraces the dynamic universe so long celebrated by American and Afro-American art.

The Image of the Father in *Black Boy*

Elizabeth Ciner

Elizabeth Ciner, assistant professor of English at Carleton College in Northfield, Minnesota, writes that in Wright's struggle to become his own man, he must reject the family that stifles his growth. He specifically works to reject the path of his own father, whom he was neither able to trust nor admire as a child. As Wright matures, he seeks less for a father to replace the one he has lost, and more for a way to be like a father himself, someone he sees as a person who has control, not over others, but over himself.

"If I were asked what is the one, overall symbol or image gained from my living that most nearly represents what I feel to be the essence of American life," Richard Wright wrote in 1942, "I'd say it is that of a man struggling mightily . . . for self-possession." The struggle of the individual for self-possession, which is a struggle to be fully human and free, is the strongest unifying element in Wright's work. . . .

For Wright, internal freedom is contingent upon one's ability to make uncoerced choices. The internally free person is a self-assertive, self-controlled individual operating autonomously in the world. Not someone known by others ("The white South said it knew 'niggers,' and I was what the white South called a 'nigger,'" Wright writes in *Black Boy*), not an object owned by another, the self-possessed person is his own master. And knowing who he is, the self-possessed person can look critically at (is not overwhelmed by) the society in which he finds himself, often taking the initiative needed to transform that society. . . .

The form the struggle for self-possession most often takes

Excerpted from Elizabeth Ciner, "Richard Wright's Struggles with Fathers," in *Myths and Realities*, edited by James C. Trotman (New York: Garland, 1988). Reprinted by permission of the publisher. (References in the original have been omitted in this reprint.)

in Wright's work is a struggle to achieve adulthood (or man-hood, since all but one of Wright's protagonists are male), and there are both personal and historical reasons for this. Keneth Kinnamon isolates "four basic facts of Wright's youth—his racial status, his poverty, the disruption of his family, and his faulty education," all of which he claims "left ineradicable scars [on Wright's] psyche and deeply influenced his thought" as well as providing "much of the subject matter of his early writings." Kinnamon's four basic facts, however, are aspects, of a more general autobiographical fact which is that Wright saw himself as locked in combat with his family. Sometimes literally and more often metaphorically, Wright believed family members tried to beat and train out of him "a kind of consciousness, a mode of being that the way of life about [him] had said could not be, must not be." In the autobiography Wright sees his relatives as enemies who, if they could, would choke off his desire to know, to do, to be, starving him not only physically but also intellectually, emotionally and spiritually.

Wright was clearest about his feelings towards his family in discussions on the autobiography. When he said, for instance, "I wrote the book to tell a series of incidents stringing through my childhood, but the main desire was to render a judgement on my environment," he meant *his* environment. So little of the autobiography concerns itself with the white South that an understanding of Wright's critique of racism and of the white racist South depends on understanding not only what they, the whites, "do" to Richard, but also what his family does to Richard. Having accepted (for whatever reasons) the terms of racism, "the static and closed order," family members become accomplices of and agents for the State. Attempting to access the degree to which racism could and did damage human beings, Wright is not interested in cherishing but in exposing what lay at the heart of his own upbringing, the attempts of his family to prevent him from ever growing up.

Of course if Wright's family did not want him to be adult as he defined it, neither did the larger society. As Addison Gayle, Jr. points out, by the time of the Civil War, a "language system" had already evolved in America which "serve[d] the twin purposes of rationalizing slavery and binding the slave mentally to the slavocracy." Both the rationalizing and the binding depended to a large degree on an analogy that equated black men and women with children. "Not content with merely enslaving black men, Americans undertook the task of stripping them of all semblance of humanity . . . reducing the man to the status of child." The rationalizations were pristine in their simplicity: If black slaves were overgrown children, then white slave owners could pretend that no real loss of freedom had occurred; they were merely beneficent parents whose wayward children required constant supervision. Those slaves who did assert themselves, who were neither loyal nor tractable, who seemed indifferent or hostile to "parental" authority and guidance, were not men and women rebelling, convinced they were complete human beings whose rights even whites must respect, but rather boys and girls who had not yet learned their lessons, or dangerous beasts, savage children in grownups' bodies. Black people from this vantage point might be biologically adult, but they were not mature morally, intellectually, or socially. By definition, if you were black, you could not possibly act like an adult, and whites worked hard to make this definition a reality, punishing and redefining all acts of self-assertion.

Although clearly the legend sketched here is but one of a number of potent legends created about blacks by whites, it is one that, given his feelings about his own family, appealed to Wright. In some ways this is what is most obvious about Wright's work. Throughout the fiction characters are blocked from reaching maturity. When they act like adults——when they try to protect their families, for instance, or improve their farms, or advance in their jobs—their actions are interpreted by whites as trying to "act white." The titles of Wright's first three published works, *Uncle Tom's Children*, *Native Son*, and *Black Boy*, contain references to non-adults; only posthumously do we find anything so positive as the title *Eight Men*, and even in that work the manhood of all but one of the characters is at issue. Black males are perpetually "boys" in the eyes of "the Man" in Wright's world. And to be a boy is to be a "non-man," says Wright, a being "that knew vaguely that it was human but felt that it was not."

REJECTING HIS FATHER'S PATH

While it is certainly true, as Donald B. Gibson asserts, that the "burden of the whole of the first chapter of *Black Boy* is a recital of examples of parental rejection providing an explanation and a justification for Wright's individualism," it is also true that while his family rejects him, Richard simultaneously rejects them. Moreover, this dual rejection serves Richard: Resisting his family not only teaches him in a general way to resist white racists, it also provides a specific map for him, a way out of the fate he feels awaits him. Richard does not want anyone to dominate him—black, white, parent, teacher, relative, boss, or priest. Committed to ordering his life by his own feelings, he rejects his uncles, the school principal, and Shorty. Above all others, though, he rejects his father and his grandmother, the two people who in their opposite but to Richard equally unacceptable reactions to racism, threaten him the most. The one, his grandmother, finds solace in a stern religion she tries to impose on Richard; the other, his father, deserts his family, finding release in alcohol and adultery. Throughout the autobiography Richard acts and reacts in ways which show him trying to be very different from these two potential role models. In the end, by becoming an author, Richard succeeds.

While the autobiography opens with an attack on his grandmother, it is with Richard's father that much of the first long chapter is concerned. Mr. Wright is "forbidding," the "lawgiver in the family," a giant in front of whom Richard is awestruck. When Richard's family moves to Memphis, Richard, afraid to go into the strange city streets alone, is confined to home where he must be quiet while his father (a night porter) sleeps. One morning Richard finds himself forced to quiet a kitten whose mewing provokes his father. "'Kill the damn thing . . . Do anything, but get it away from here,'" his father commands. Immediately resentful, Richard hangs the kitten and so, Wright tells us, enjoys his "first triumph" over his father.

When Richard had hanged the kitten, his mother had warned him "'That kitten's going to get you,'" a warning Richard shrugged off, saying "'That kitten can't even breathe now.'" But Richard learns he is wrong: "My mother's words," he reports, "made it live again in my mind." Victim here of another's language, Richard experiences words as weapons, as surely as he will experience them fourteen years later when reading H.L. Mencken. As a final gesture, his mother forces him into a prayer of forgiveness—"Dear God, our father, forgive me, for I knew not what I was doing"—which perhaps for the first time links biological and spiritual fathers. Subsequent

BURYING THE FATHER

Wright's symbolic attempt to bury his father—a man who is as good as dead to him—corresponds with his attempt to ignore other members of family and society who attempt to stifle his individuality.

At the end of the first chapter he recalls his last meeting with his father in 1940, providing an exaggerated geriatric description complete with toothless mouth, white hair, bent body, glazed eyes, gnarled hands. His father was a brutalized "black peasant," "a creature of the earth" without loyalty, sentiment, tradition, joy, or despair—all in contrast to his son, who lives "on a vastly different plane of reality," who speaks a different language, and who has traveled to "undreamed-of shores of knowing." Wright's symbolic effort to bury his father corresponds to a persistent attempt to come into his own by opposing or ignoring all members of his family, who consistently try to stifle his articulation of his individuality, to inhibit his quest for freedom. Shouting joyously at the sight of a free-flying bird outside his window, Richard is rebuked in the opening scene by his younger brother with the words "'You better hush.'" His mother immediately steps in to reinforce the message: "'You stop that yelling, you hear?'" These are the first words spoken to Richard in *Black Boy*, but they reverberate in other mouths throughout the work.

From Keneth Kinnamon, "Intertextuality in Two Autobiographical Works by Richard Wright and Maya Angelou," *Belief vs. Theory in Black American Literary Criticism*, Greenwood, FL: Penkevill, 1986, p. 127.

episodes will cement the connection: When Richard complains of hunger, his mother insists that he will have to wait for God to send food because his father is gone; a preacher, "God's representative," a man also used to having his "own way," eats all the fried chicken while Richard labors unsuccessfully to finish his soup. Fathers, spiritual or biological, Richard's experience leads him to believe, satisfy their own appetites at the expense of their children.

With his father gone, Richard's mother sends him out to buy the groceries. Richard sets out "proud" and feeling "like a grownup." When he is robbed and beaten (and forced out of the house by his mother), he compensates for his youth and small size, arming himself with a big stick, defending himself first against the boys who stole from him and then against their parents who "rushed into the streets and threatened [him]: They had never seen such frenzy. For the first time in my life I shouted at grownups, telling them I would give them the same if they bothered me." Richard's victory here is a multiple one. Supplanting his father as provider of food, he triumphs over him a second time and more decisively. At the same time he triumphs over his own fear. Where Richard had been "afraid to go into the city streets alone" now he has "won" for himself the "right to the streets of Memphis."

Once free from fear, Richard quickly familiarizes himself with the adult world which has captured his father, showing himself to be his father's son. Far from home, the boy frequents a saloon, learns to drink, and is taught to proposition women. At the age of six, "[f]or a penny or a nickel I would repeat to anyone whatever was whispered to me," encouraged by the responses he got. "In my foggy, tipsy state, the reaction of the men and women to my mysterious words enthralled me. I ran from person to person, laughing, hiccoughing, spewing out filth that made them bend double with glee." Given his inclinations, why Wright does not follow in his father's footsteps is one of the mysteries of the next. Perhaps his mother's beatings are effective. Perhaps when the effects of the alcohol wear off what Richard remembers from these experiences is not the comfort of the drink but the power of his socially unacceptable language.

Richard sees his father one last time in boyhood, at the home of his father's mistress. He recoils from the encounter for reasons he cannot make clear to himself:

> We left. I had the feeling that I had had to do with something unclean. Many times in the years after that the image of my father and the strange woman, their faces lit by the dancing flames, would surge up in my imagination so vivid and strong that I felt I could reach out and touch it; I would stare at it, feeling that it possessed some vital meaning which always eluded me.

According to Albert Stone, the fire "represents the sexual passion which separates and unites father, mother, and mistress and which likewise includes the child who, looking into the coals, sees himself an unconscious participant in the sexual drama." But as a child, all Richard knows is that he is on one side of a room, his father is on the other, between them is "a bright fire that blazed in a grate," and the gap between them is not as wide as Richard would have it be. Even not knowing what other life is possible for him, Richard instinctively rejects the narrow and degraded life his father has chosen.

A Symbolic Search for the Father

Carl Brignano claims that Wright was searching for a father and that the search "was a real one," although symbolically the search expresses itself as "a search for Negro dignity, economic opportunity, and social acceptance in a racially integrated South." More to the point perhaps, Wright appears to be searching for a way to be a father, a person in power if not over others than at least over himself. His father's fire attracts Richard, but his father's life, finally, does not. Wright is emphatic on this point in the chapter's final paragraphs:

> A quarter of a century was to elapse between the time when I saw my father sitting with the strange woman and the time I was to see him again . . . a sharecropper, clad in ragged overalls, holding a muddy hoe in his gnarled, veined hands—a quarter of a century during which my mind and consciousness had become so greatly and violently altered that when I tried to talk to him I realized that, though ties of blood made us kin, though I could see a shadow of my face in his face, though there was an echo of my voice in his voice, we were forever strangers, speaking a different language, living on vastly distant planes of reality.

Whatever Wright has become it is not his father. From this point in the narrative, the older Wright drops out, his ghost, so to speak, emerging at the end of *Black Boy* to haunt Richard when he returns to Memphis as a young man. Memphis, for Wright, is the city his father "had gone to . . . seeking life." But his father "had failed in the city; a black peasant whose life had been hopelessly snarled in the city, and who had at last fled the city," that same city in whose "burning arms" Richard is "lifted" and "borne . . . toward alien and undreamed-of shores of knowing.". . .

After his father's desertion, Richard, his brother, and his mother return to Granny's house. There Richard meets the young schoolteacher Ella who boards with the family. When he asks her about the books she reads, Ella, who knows Granny forbids novels, attempts to placate Richard by closing her book and whispering to him *Bluebeard and His Seven Wives.* Richard is "[e]nchanted and enthralled" by the story. "My imagination blazed," Wright writes. But just as Ella is about to finish, "when my interest was keenest, when I was lost to the world around me," Granny steps out on the porch and puts an end to the story, telling Ella, "'I want none of that Devil stuff in my house!'" warning Richard, "'You're going to burn in hell.'"

The story is indeed the Devil's stuff, about Bluebeard, a satanic figure if ever there was one, and it is precisely the story Richard wants to hear: "Ella's whispered story of deception and murder had been the first experience in my life that had elicited from me a total emotional response." Richard's life is given symbolic form through the story; deprived of it he is deprived of a way to come to grips with his life through literature. But as the subsequent scene shows, Richard not only empathizes with Bluebeard's wives but also with Bluebeard who through deception and violence achieves his unlawful desires. Within days, Richard mounts an ingenious attack on Granny, this one a symbolic and linguistic assault.

Richard and his brother are taking baths in two tubs of water under the watchful eyes of Granny. Splashing water, flinging suds at one another, they ignore Granny's scolding until she puts down her knitting and calls Richard to her:

> "Bend over," she ordered.
>
> I stooped and she scrubbed my anus. My mind was in a sort of daze, midway between daydreaming and thinking. Then, before I knew it, words—words whose meaning I did not fully know—had slipped out of my mouth.
>
> "When you get through, kiss back there," I said, the words rolling softly but unpremeditately.

Pandemonium ensues. With eyes "blazing," Granny shoves Richard from her and beats him with a towel she is holding. Naked, he runs screaming from the house as his mother hurries from her bed. Granny, close to hysterics, reports on what "that black little Devil" has done, and Richard's mother takes up both towel and chase.

Much in the form of this scene looks back to the opening scene of the autobiography; its content, though, derives from Richard's early experiences with language: words like "enthralled" and "dazed" recall his saloon experiences while "soap" and "scrub" attach themselves to an episode which involved Richard scribbling obscene words on windows with a soap cake. None of the characters makes any of these connections. Granny's explanation holds sway: She "said emphatically that she knew who had ruined me," Richard reports, "that she knew I learned about 'foul practices' from reading Ella's books."

Granny, who distrusts stories because they are fictions and hence lies is wrong about Ella and foul practices only in

fact. Fictionally speaking Granny is right; stories can be the
Devil's work and this one has been, providing Richard with
what he needed to attack Granny for interfering with his
pleasure in hearing the story. While Richard called the story
one of deception and murder, it is also a story of sexual per-
version, of foul practices.

When Richard says that Granny "knew who had ruined"
him by teaching him "foul practices," the implication is
clearly sexual, and Wright is effecting a comic reversal with
Ella becoming the seducer and Richard the one seduced. The
language of the Bluebeard scene itself is sexual—feelings well
up, things seem to throb, Richard feels his body ablaze with
excitement. Referring back to the word-play Richard in-
dulged in the first chapter, this language also recalls
Richard's encounter with his father and the strange woman,
the incident he came away from feeling as if he had had
something "to do with something unclean." Richard's
choice of a sexual gesture towards Granny and Wright's
adoption of sexually laden language in the description of
Richard's responses to literature show Richard open to the
same kinds of impulses his father is open to. But Richard
will channel those impulses differently, the differentness
demonstrating his discontinuity with his father. Initiated as
he is in the Bluebeard scene not into the world of the flesh
but into the world of story-telling, Richard's impulses serve
another god.

Richard's responses to the story are not unlike the responses of an initiate, a convert, and they parallel Granny's
responses to religion. Where she sees angels, he sees magical presences. His books generate in him a transcendent experience and momentarily blot out reality, making him feel
"lost to reality" and so compete with her religion in which
she feels dead to the world. Richard in fact adopts his grandmother's terms—devil, evil, hell—and then transforms
them. From Granny's point of view, the dreamy schoolteacher is "evil," books are the "devil's stuff," Richard's desire to know, "the devil's work," and Richard himself "a little black devil" who surely is "going to burn in hell." That is
all right with Richard, who appropriates the terms; he
"burns to learn to read novels" and "tortures his mother" as
a good devil ought "to define every strange word" he comes
upon, because he has learned from Granny . . . that words
are the "gateway to a forbidden and enchanting land."

No One's Son

In the course of *Black Boy* what is implicit in the Bluebeard-bathtub sequence is made explicit: if Richard is a devil, then the saint is someone who has cut him or her self off from life; if his acts are evil, then being good is akin to being dead; if he is headed for hell, then heaven is a static place where nothing much happens. Within this framework, novels *are* the devil's work, opening up possibilities for the individual in a society which depends for its existence on those possibilities being denied, a society, furthermore, which works to deny that any life other than that proscribed is possible.

Richard's reaction to this proscription is complex and germinal. At the age of twelve, having promised Granny "to pray hard," Richard goes up to his room every afternoon, "but everything I could think of saying seemed silly." Failing even at writing hymn verses, Richard claims that "the Holy Ghost was simply nowhere near me." The Holy Ghost may be absent, but not so Richard's muse: "One day while killing my hour of prayer," Wright writes, he is inspired to write an Indian love story. "I had made something," he writes, "no matter how bad it was; and it was mine." Paradoxically, then, Richard's first work of art emerges under the pressure of Granny's religiosity. As if he had taken his directions from her, Richard creates not prayer but exactly the kind of work Granny burns, becoming exactly what she had feared he would become.

If the crucial difference between Richard and his father has been that the son succumbs not to passion but to art, then the difference between Richard and his grandmother is that while she uses religion to withdraw from a world she finds intolerable, he will seek a way through words, as Wright would put it, to alter his relationship to his environment and thereby prove himself to be a free man. From Richard's point of view, Granny and others like her fly to religion as an answer to the pain of their existence. He flees the South, however, so that he may find the words to describe the life he has known, and in describing that life create for himself (and for other) a new one. Writing stories is finally a religious activity for Richard, writing redeeming him as religion redeems Granny. While Granny's religion frees her from the world, Richard's frees him into it.

His choice of professions, then, is no accident: becoming a writer, he becomes at once an author, creator, and artist, and this may be said to specifically solve his problems. As a writer of books, he creates new worlds and thereby competes with Granny's God, the source of her authority and Richard's spiritual father; as an autobiographer, he engenders himself and so displaces his biological father. Recreating his world and himself for us, as he sees it, Wright even outwits his political fathers, white men of the South, who never imagine a black boy *could* become a writer. Wright does become one though, and in so doing transforms himself, permanently altering his fate and status. No longer a native son doomed to an obscure and deadened existence, he becomes Richard Wright.

CHAPTER 3

The Black Experience

READINGS ON
BLACK BOY

Wright's Autobiography Becomes a Universal Story of Black Experience

Yoshinobu Hakutani

Professor of English at Kent State University in Ohio and author and editor of numerous scholarly collections, Yoshinobu Hakutani explains that *Black Boy* is an eloquent expression of social and cultural views, an autobiography that portrays experiences with naturalistic objectivity, rather than personal intimacy. Racial discourse is presented through imagery, dialogue, and Wright's impersonal stance, as he not only describes the environment of his youth, but passes judgment on it.

Black Boy is acclaimed not only as the finest autobiography written by an African American, but as one of the finest autobiographies written in America. Indeed, many American autobiographies, are ethnic. As *Black Boy* discusses the experience of an African American youth who grew up in the South, Theodore Dreiser's *Dawn* treats the life struggle that the son of a German immigrant faced in the North. Benjamin Franklin's *Autobiography* is not ethnic in the usual sense of the word, but his life exemplifies the American dream of the poor boy who made good in Pennsylvania, an English colony. What these autobiographies have in common is not only an eloquent portrayal of early life, but a poignant expression of social and cultural views.

Unlike Dreiser's *Dawn* and Franklin's *Autobiography*, *Black Boy* features a narrator who takes such an impersonal attitude that the work may not seem like a usual autobiography. As W.E.B. Du Bois noted, there is in *Black Boy* a gen-

Excerpted from Yoshinobu Hakutani, "Racial Discourse and Self-Creation: Richard Wright's *Black Boy*," in *Teaching American Ethnic Literatures*, edited by John R. Maitino and David R. Peck (Albuquerque: University of New Mexico Press, 1996). Reprinted by permission of the publisher. (References in the original have been omitted in this reprint.)

uine paucity of personal love or affection expressed toward Wright's mother. Wright does express his awe and wonder at his suffering mother, but he is unable to understand the reason that she was deserted by her husband, broken by paralysis, and overwhelmed by every unimaginable circumstance she had to face. His reaction therefore is intellectual rather than personal. By contrast, in *Dawn* the narrator's wonder at his suffering mother is tinged with personal sorrow and sympathy. Wright's intention in *Black Boy* seems to have been to portray his experience with naturalistic objectivity, rather than firsthand intimacy.

By the time he wrote *Black Boy*, Wright had become a literary naturalist who adopts a milieu from life and projects characters that act in accordance with the milieu. The naturalist records, without comment or interpretation, what actually happens. If Wright regarded himself as a fictional persona in *Black Boy*, he would be less concerned either with his own life or with his own point of view. The focus of his interest in the book would be on the events that occurred outside of his life. It is understandable, then, that Wright's account of his own life would not be entirely authentic. One might even suspect that Wright's self-portrait would abound with fictional accounts, and in fact many differences between *Black Boy* and his life have been pointed out. One reviewer's objection to the book as autobiography is based on discrepancies found between Wright's accounts in the book and "The Ethics of Living Jim Crow." In addition, Wright refers in *Black Boy* to his mother as a cook "in the kitchens of the white folks" and describes her as less intellectual than she really was. In fact, Ella Wilson, his mother, before her marriage to his father, was considerably well educated and taught school. Edwin R. Embree, an African American writer himself, who was closely acquainted with Wright's youth and early literary career, testifies that Wright's mother was light brown and good-looking, and that book learning enabled her to obtain teaching jobs at twenty-five dollars a month.

These discrepancies, however, are not a major reason for calling *Black Boy* a fictionalized autobiography. Even though parts of the book are fictional, it is largely autobiographical and should not be equated with a novel. No one for a moment can overlook the fact that *Black Boy* portrays Wright himself, and if the work also concerns others, their lives are necessarily intertwined with his life. But the most important feature which distinguishes *Black Boy* as autobiography is Wright's intention to use the young self as a mask. The attitudes and sentiments expressed by the young Wright are not totally his own, but represent the responses of those he called "the voiceless Negro boys" of the South. Such a device makes *Black Boy* a unique autobiography, just as a similar technique makes *Native Son* a unique novel. Speaking of that novel, Wright says, in "How 'Bigger' Was Born," that Bigger Thomas is a conscious composite portrait of numerous African American individuals he knew in his life.

STYLE AND ARTISTRY TELL A BITTER TRUTH

What makes *Black Boy* not only a unique autobiography but, perhaps, the most influential racial discourse in America is its style and artistry. What impresses many readers about the book is that it tells bitter truth about life. Wright cannot be criticized for his subject matter, because he is not responsible for the world he had not made. Above all, *Black Boy* impresses the reader because Wright remains an artist throughout the text. As in his best fiction, his language, unlike the language of a typical naturalist, is terse, lucid, and vivid; his presentation is moving and dramatic. Horace R. Cayton, a sociologist who intimately knew Wright's method, quotes him as saying: "I try to float these facts on a sea of emotion, to drive them home with some degree of artistic power, as much as humanly possible. . . . I want people to enjoy my books but I want them to be moved and conditioned by them." In short, a bitter man can be a great artist as well.

The poetic passages characteristic of *Black Boy* thus convey the narrator's various emotional responses to his life in the South. Such language often forms a blend of disparate images that are unified only by the intensity of feeling. Some images—"spotted, black-and-white horses," "long straight rows of red and green vegetables," "the yellow, dreaming waters of the Mississippi River"—all suggest a harmony of nature and society. Others—"the crying strings of wild geese" and "a solitary ant carrying a burden upon a mysterious journey"—allude to racial anxiety and tension. Still others—"a [tortured] delicate, blue-pink crawfish that huddled fearfully in the mudsill of a rusty tin can" and "a chicken [leaping] about blindly after its neck had been snapped by a quick twist of my father's wrist"—depict cruelty and sadism.

In these images Wright interpolates such a statement as: "Each event spoke with a cryptic tongue. And the moments of living slowly revealed their coded meanings." This, however, does not necessarily signal that each of the images evoked has a point-for-point correspondence with a specific event in reality. Wright might or might not have intended "a brace of mountainlike, spotted, black-and-white horses clopping down a dusty road" to allude to miscegenation. The same is true of comparing the chicken leaping with its neck cut off to a victim of racial violence. Wright's imagery often appears unrelated to actuality, because facts of life are elevated to a higher level of consciousness and sensibility. "The relationship between reality and the artistic image," he says in "Blueprint for Negro Writing," "is not always direct and simple. The imaginative conception of a historical period will not be a carbon copy of reality. Image and emotion possess a logic of their own."

In establishing his own world, then, Wright is able to shape the images at will. He knew what hunger and hatred meant in his youth and he had learned to live with them, but he now had a new hunger for the freedom of the mind. "I seemed forever condemned," he writes, "ringed by walls." This image of imprisonment recurs throughout the book. He remembers that at four he tried to burn down his grandmother's house by setting fire to the white curtains. "I crossed restlessly to the window," he recalls, "and pushed back the long fluffy white curtains—which I had been forbidden to touch—and looked yearningly out into the empty street." As he grew older and was allowed to play in the street, he saw one day a host of chained convicts, all black, dressed in the black-and-white striped clothing, a spectacle that at once reminded him of zebras confined in the zoo.

In addition to imagery, dialogue dramatizes his racial discourse. Wright is at his best when much of the episode is interlaced with revealing dialogue. The narrator deliberately creates a scene where two individuals, usually the young Wright and an opponent, confront each other with an exchange of laconic statements. These remarks not only reveal the gullibility of an antagonist, but compel the reader to identify with the narrator. Wright once encountered in an elevator a black youth who exposed his buttocks for a white man to kick so that he might earn a quarter. Wright says he felt "no anger or hatred, only disgust and loathing," and that he confronted this youth:

"How in God's name can you do that?"
"I needed a quarter and I got it," he said soberly, proudly.
"But a quarter can't pay you for what he did to you," I said.
"Listen, nigger," he said to me, "my ass is tough and quarters is scarce."

At thirteen, when Wright was forced to seek a job as a house-boy, a white woman, a prospective employer looking for an "honest" black boy, gave him an interview:

"Now, boy, I want to ask you one question and I want you to tell me the truth," she said.
"Yes, ma'am," I said, all attention.
"Do you steal?" she asked me seriously.
I burst into a laugh, then checked myself.
"What's so damn funny about that?" she asked.
"Lady, if I was a thief, I'd never tell anybody."

Wright also heightens his racial discourse with irony. The statement by an antagonist inadvertently betrays more than he wants to say, or there is a marked contrast between what he wants to say and what his words mean to the reader. For example, Wright's boss at an optical company in Jackson, Mississippi, who originally came from Illinois, professed himself unprejudiced and boasted that he wanted to "break a colored boy into the optical trade." The white man, how-ever, cautioned the young Wright: "You're going to have a chance to learn a trade. But remember to keep your head. Remember you're black." Ironically, the white man's warn-ing suggests that rebelling against the Jim Crow law, as Wright was resolved to do, would be considered insane. At times Wright's irony verges on humor. On another occasion, he went up to a hotel room to wait on a white prostitute and a white man lying naked on the bed. The presence of a black man in this situation would awaken in the white people no sense of shame since he was in no way considered "human." The prostitute asked Wright to buy some liquor for them, and slid out of bed and walked naked across the floor. As she searched for her purse, Wright naturally watched her. He was immediately warned by the white man: "Keep your eyes where they belong if you want to be healthy!" Such a state-ment reveals that a black boy is regarded as subhuman or abnormal in the eyes of white men and women of the South.

WRIGHT'S IMPERSONAL STANCE

These rhetorical skills enable Wright to develop his racial discourse with vigor. As an artist he detaches himself from the scene he depicts; above all, he remains a judicious observer. His aim is to bring home his hard-won conviction that racial problems stem not so much from the individuals involved as from a system inherited from the past. At times, the white race is as much a victim as the black race. Many episodes show that the kind of sympathy white southerners felt for black people was nothing more than racial condescension. Although white people in the South considered themselves decent, compassionate human beings, they had a deep-seated, unconscious attitude reminiscent of Aunt Sally's response to Huck Finn. When Huck reports that a steamboat has just blown out a cylinder head down the river and killed a black man, she replies nonchalantly: "Well, it's lucky; because sometimes people do get hurt. . . ."

The impersonality of *Black Boy* can be explained in another way. Since the narrator is a spokesman for the voiceless black youths in America, he must be objective and scientific in his observations. This book, though not intended as such, is a convincing sociological study. Like sociology, the study not only analyzes a social problem but offers a solution to the problem it treats. Wright explores the ways in which African American life in the South was determined by environment, and, to borrow Émile Zola's words in "The Experimental Novel," he wants to "disengage the determinism of human and social phenomena so that we may one day control and direct these phenomena." Like Zola, Wright makes his investigation systematic and unbiased. Such writing therefore deals with the specific social forces in the environment of a black boy: white racism, black society, and black family.

James Baldwin assailed Wright for the belief that "in Negro life there exists no tradition, no field of manners, no possibility of ritual or intercourse." Unlike Baldwin, who grew up in a highly religious black community in Harlem, Wright witnessed in the Deep South "the essential bleakness of black life in America." The central issue, however, is whether such human traits as, in Wright's words, "tenderness, love, honor, loyalty, and the capacity to remember" are innate in the African American tradition, as Baldwin says, or are "fostered, won, struggled and suffered for," as Wright believed. Wright says elsewhere that he wrote *Black Boy* "to tell a series of incidents strung through my childhood, but the main desire was to render a judgment on my environment. . . . That judgment was this: the environment the South creates is too small to nourish human beings, especially Negro human beings." Wright, therefore, squarely places the burden of proof upon white society, contending with enough evidence and justification given in *Black Boy* that the absence of such human qualities in black people as tenderness and love stemmed from years of white oppression.

Not only did white racism succeed in separating black and white people, but it had devastating effects on black life. Critics, both black and white, have complained that Wright in *Black Boy* lacks racial pride. It is true that he is critical of the black community in the South, but it is not true that he places the blame on the black community itself. His intention is to show that a racist system produced the way of life that was forced on black people. In terms of social determinism, *Black Boy* provides a literary experiment to demonstrate uniformity in black behavior under the influence of social forces.

Most black people, he admits, do adjust to their environment for survival. But in so doing they lose individuality, self-respect, and dignity. For Wright, the circumstances in which they find themselves damage their personalities, and this in turn results in various forms of hypocritical, erratic, and despicable behavior. In addressing white men's sexual exploitation of black women, Wright is as critical of black women as of white men, because he believed black women expect and readily condone white men's behavior. Once a black maid, slapped playfully on her buttocks by a white nightwatchman, told the indignant Wright, a witness to the incident: "'They never get any further with us than that, if we don't want 'em to.'" Understandably, such portraits of black people made some readers feel that Wright unduly deprived black people of their personal honor and dignity. But Wright explains: "I began to marvel at how smoothly the black boys acted out the roles that the white race had mapped out for them. Most of them were not conscious of living a special, separate, stunted way of life."

COMPROMISE AND SELF-CREATION

In Wright's view, this absence of individuality and self-awareness among black people in the South often leads to the compromise of their character, as also shown in *The Long Dream*, Wright's last novel. Individually, Fishbelly and his father in that novel are powerless in asserting themselves. Although they are not forced or coerced to cooperate with white police, their greed often compromises their moral integrity. Wright presents them as fully aware that their illicit political connections will make them as wealthy as white people.

Structurally, the young Wright's observations on white racism and black life buttress the central theme of *Black Boy*, self-creation. In "Blueprint for Negro Writing," Wright argues that the "theme for Negro writers will rise from understanding the meaning of their being transplanted from a 'savage' to a 'civilized' culture in all of its social, political, economic, and emotional implications." In *Black Boy*, his chief aim is to show how this youth, whom the South called a "nigger," surmounted his obstacles in the civilized culture. The most painful stance he took in this struggle was to be an intense individualist; he created selfhood and exerted his will at the risk of annihilation. Both black and white communities imposed crushing circumstances upon him, but no matter how unbearable his problems were, he refused to compromise. Thus, Wright's logic becomes clear: only under such pressure does one discover one's self. For others, this process of self-creation might have been aided by chance, but for Wright "it should be a matter of plan."

The reader could be puzzled by this youth's individuality and fortitude if the seed of manhood had not been sown in the child. *Black Boy*, however, contains ample evidence of the child's precocity and independence. Wright's earlier self is revealed even to the point of betraying his vanity. When he moved to his grandmother's house after his family was deserted by his father, Wright took pride in telling the timid children of the new neighborhood about his train ride, his Mississippi cruise, and his escape from the orphanage. Moreover, the young child is presented as a rebel who refused to compromise with the dictates of society and family. Once, he was dismayed to find out that the man who had beaten a black boy was not the boy's father. Although Wright was told by his mother that he was "too young to understand," he responded with a resolution: "'I'm not going to let anybody beat me.'"

As early as twelve, Wright held "a sense of the world that was mine and mine alone, a notion . . . that no education could ever alter, a conviction that the meaning of living came only when one was struggling to wring meaning out of meaningless suffering." His decision to leave the South seven years later, his final action, was based upon such conviction, as if the seed of manhood had already been in the child. Without mental companionship to rely on, he withdrew and turned inward like the anti-hero of an existentialist novel. In his recoil, he had once again discovered that the revelation of all truths must come through the action and anguish of the self. It was at this point in his ordeal that he came in contact with the writings of American realists such as H.L. Mencken, Theodore Dreiser, Sinclair Lewis, and Sherwood Anderson. It was their ideas, he says, that literally delivered his brooding sensibility to a brighter horizon, a vision that "America could be shaped nearer to the hearts of those who lived in it." He also at this time decided to head North to discover for himself that one could live with dignity and determine one's own destiny. Because he knew he could not make the world, he sought to make things happen within him and caught a sense of freedom, and in so doing he discovered the new world.

Black Boy Is Appropriate Reading for Young Adults

Maryemma Graham and Jerry W. Ward Jr.

Maryemma Graham, associate professor of English and African American studies at Northeastern University and Jerry W. Ward Jr., professor of literature at Tougaloo College, defend Black Boy *against groups that call for its censorship in schools. Graham and Ward promote its value to students in that it provides a language for the mysteries of human existence and probes issues of race and gender in the United States.*

CENSORSHIP. The word evokes the shouting down of speakers whose ideas are somehow ideologically incorrect, the destruction of printing presses, the spectacle of parents angry that school texts contain language and ideas pernicious to underaged Dick and Jane (which they already think of as ancient), bans on the exhibition of Mapplethorpe photographs, the Inquisition, special markings for motion pictures and rap compact discs, and the pyramid of books aflame. Ideas and images deemed offensive must be suppressed or hidden or destroyed. The censoring agents are either "legally" constituted policies regarding heresy, obscenity, and sedition, or instant spokespersons for community values. On the other hand, there is no reason censorship should not also bring to mind the idea of taking a census, of counting heads and thus accounting for population, for in classical Latin *censor* refers to one of two officials who took the census. It is profitable for readers of Richard Wright's *Black Boy*, either the first edition of 1945 or the unexpurgated Library of America edition of 1991 to consider options in positioning Wright's autobiography. The book might be suppressed in public school curricula on the grounds that it

Reprinted from Maryemma Graham and Jerry W. Ward Jr., "*Black Boy* (*American Hunger*): Freedom to Remember," in *Censored Books: Critical Viewpoints*, edited by Nicholas J. Karolides, Lee Burgess, and John M. Kean (Metuchen, NJ: Scarecrow Press, 1993), by permission of the publisher.

is morally (and politically) "dangerous." The greater danger is nurturing cultural illiteracy by denying students the opportunity to learn why *Black Boy* might free the mind to remember what the hypocrisy of censorship would conceal.

Recognizing the ambiguous reception that might be accorded *Black Boy*, we accepted the invitation to prepare a rationale or defense of the book. That the book is an autobiography, a record of childhood and youth, is crucial. Recreating and inscribing himself in a particularized moment of American history from angles available to an African American male, Wright did not intend to corrupt, scandalize, or blaspheme but rather to illustrate how obscene was denial of access to full participation in the democratic process by law, custom, and the practice of race. One need not prepare, except as a supplement, a rationale for *Black Boy;* the autobiography embodies its own defense.

Discovering the book's rationale against censorship does require the effort to understand that the primal causes in the making of the book were Wright's analytic intelligence and the cultivated hell the United States was for black Americans between 1900 and 1945, and to some extent continues to be despite the illusion of progress. The rationale for the autobiography is the same we attribute to any work we conclude is liberating; it provides a necessary language for the mysteries of *human existence* that manifest themselves in the rhetoric of dream and nightmare.

The claim that *Black Boy* is liberating, even mythical, is not to be taken as an assertion that the book explains much more than the universal potentials of the person who is socialized to be black and male in a racist society. Richard Wright selected those he deemed most representative of his own life experiences from a range of such potentials. At the risk of being simple, we must remind readers that *Black Boy* speaks specifically for Wright. And Wright speaks specifically for a very distinct community, a fact that he made explicit in his January 26, 1940 acceptance speech before the Springarn Award Committee. At the beginning of the speech, Wright said:

> It is with a deep sense of responsibility that I accept the Springarn Medal. I accept it in the name of the stalwart, enduring millions of Negroes whose fate and destiny I have sought to depict, in terms of narrative and scene, in imaginative fiction. It cannot be otherwise, for they are my people, and my writing—which is my life and which carries my con-

victions—attempts to mirror their struggles for freedom during these troubled days.

> [from a typescript of the speech given to Maryemma Graham by Julia Wright]

These were and still are powerful words, and they should remind us that Wright saw the world through his own terrifying set of experiences, just as most writers relate to their experiences.

AMERICAN OPTIMISM BETRAYED

The significance of the book as commentary on other black American males changes according to a reader's affinities, social experiences, associations and knowledge of literary conventions. As Ralph Ellison informed readers, *Black Boy* is Richard Wright's blues. Attempts to condemn or censor Wright's autobiography for its negative portrayal of black males and females are perhaps misreadings of a hypertextual kind, insufficiently attentive to genre and to the "facts" of race and gender at the time of the book's composition. To remove the book from the material complexity in which it was formed serves to further conceal the dynamics of the specific historical and intellectual processes which inform the work's production and transmission. It is precisely the "facts" of race and gender in the United States that help us probe the sociohistorical matrix of this important work.

On the other hand, autobiography is not sociology, however rich its sociological implications might be. The abused male, playing subject to his own objectification, has the options of *accommodating* oppression, *becoming* the destructive and self-destructive rebel, or *resisting* through a spiraling quest for the safe space where integrity, balance, and wholeness might be achieved. In Wright's first published novel, *Native Son*, Bigger becomes the destructive and self-destructive rebel, whose quest for wholeness is accomplished through means more criminal than rational. In *Black Boy* is a record, one man's record, partially authentic and partially fictional, of the achievement of the safe space, with integrity and balance intact; it is a wholeness based on self-control and discipline. Wright exercises other options for the recorded memory of his own life than those he had chosen for *Native Son*.

The rather graphic portrait of an abused male child, together with his presentation of his parents' failure to fulfill their responsibility, creates sufficient justification for Wright's predisposition toward extreme individualism, self-reliance, and non-conformity. His growth experiences stress the need for self-discovery, about himself, as the representative voice of all black boys and girls, and about the society in which he lived. It can be argued that as an artist Wright highlighted the negativity of *accommodating* and *becoming* in order to strengthen the act of *transcending resistance* that is *Black Boy*.

The book is a trace of Wright's exploitation of outsideness, Wright's prowess in manipulating language and its codes. Part of the success of this manipulation is demonstrated by his ability to subvert the discourse of the dominant culture and bring it under the terms of his own control. Nowhere is this clearer than in his strategy for borrowing books from the segregated public library in Memphis. Not only does he "forge" (the dual meaning seems intentional) his own notes to borrow the books, but he names himself "nigger" to insure his success:

> That afternoon I addressed myself to forging a note. Now, what were the names of books written by H.L. Mencken? I did not know any of them. I finally wrote what I thought would be a foolproof note: *Dear Madam: Will you please let this nigger boy*—I used the word "nigger" to make the librarian feel that I could not possibly be the author of the note—*have some books by H.L. Mencken?* I forged the white man's name.

Using quite personal angles, Wright insured that readers would honestly confront what is endemic in a closed society.

Black Boy establishes its one justification in the sense that George Orwell's *1984*, Aldous Huxley's *Brave New World*, and Ray Bradbury's *Fahrenheit 451* do. These books invite us to imaginatively recreate the experience of living within closed systems. It tells us much about social breakdown and disorder in American life with a vividness sociological writing cannot provide. It valorizes the enduring importance of slave narrative, for example, as a genre for understanding the insights and aspirations of the oppressed, a genre that has always named the lie upon which American society has and continues to batten: the beautiful and truly noble democratic theories of life, liberty and the pursuit of happiness. The reality for a substantial number of Americans has been death, unfreedom, and the flight from despair. *Black Boy* performs the Latinate role of accounting.

Black Boy is a critique of American optimism betrayed. In the context of Wright's autobiography, the myth of optimism in democracy and what some members of the democratic state decide it is important for other members to never know and experience. What is it in *Black Boy* that is so horrible that the book should be censored? The accusing finger directed at democratic principles that failed?

CONTEMPORARY REACTION AGAINST *BLACK BOY*

The reaction of Pete Trussell of Jackson, Mississippi, to *Native Son* provides clues for anticipating reactions to *Black Boy*. Let us assume that Trussell is one of a growing body of parents who make censorship challenges, part of a movement well documented in the American Library Association's Office of Intellectual Freedom survey of secondary school librarians for the years 1986-89. In his letter to the editor of *The Clarion-Ledger* (February 24, 1992), Trussell is concerned that the National Endowment for the Humanities awarded a grant to the Mississippi Authority for Educational Television to produce a documentary on Wright's life. Wright, after all, authored books that included "profanity and racially offensive language," "accounts of fornication and adultery," "alcohol abuse by minors," and "sympathy toward the Communist Party." And Trussell feels "very strongly about our underage children being required to read material of this type in public schools." The scenario of attempted censorship ended well, according to *The Clarion-Ledger* of May 19, 1992.

> Pete Trussell . . . objected to *Native Son*, by Richard Wright, being required reading for all 10th-graders because of foul language and violence.
>
> Trussell, whose daughter Jennifer, attends Wingfield High School, first objected to the novel in November. Since then, a committee of parents, students, teachers and principals have reviewed the book and recommended it remain on the required reading list but that it be taught in the 11th grade.
>
> Trussell was told [by the Jackson School Board] that district policy allows students to choose an alternative to a book they find offensive.

In this instance, all freedoms—the freedom to read, the freedom to object, the freedom to choose—were preserved. Jennifer may have chosen to read *Gone With the Wind*.

What is potentially offensive in *Black Boy* may be profane language and violence, but the function of profanity and vio-

A NEGRO REVOLUTION OF LETTERS

Writer Sinclair Lewis describes a number of other books published concurrently with Black Boy *that suggest a revolution of sorts among the African American community, which seeks to be known not as a "colored people," but as "people."*

There has recently appeared, at the same time as *Black Boy*, the skilled and important report by the secretary of the National Association for the Advancement of Colored People, my friend Walter White, upon what has been happening to American Negro soldiers in our camps at home and in England, and at the battlefront in Italy and Africa. There are in this report numerous exact incidents of Jim Crowism lugged into our Army of Democracy. The main impressions that come out of reading it are the continued segregation of Negro soldiers from their white comrades in Red Cross clubs and even in adjacent villages, and the fact that, except for a few sectors in which Negroes have brilliantly fought and flown, they have been restricted to labor units instead of being trusted as fighters.

Soldier workers, lugging supplies ashore during landings, or driving trucks or repairing roads under fire, get killed just as frequently—it may even be just as painfully—as the white fighters, but there is no credit in it. They are expected to live like dogs and not even to die as heroes.

The assertions of Mr. White are amply backed up by a woman, a white woman, a woman from a Navy family, in another just-issued book, *Jim Crow Grows Up*, by Ruth Danenhower Wilson.

If there had appeared only these three books, these three disturbing Border Incidents, they would still be enough to make the wise observer fear that a revolution in Negro affairs is threatened. But one may go beyond them to a score of other related books published in the past three years, and if America can possibly take the time from its study of comic strips to discover even the titles of these books, it may realize that this is a revolution, and that it is not coming—it is here.

The unwritten manifesto of this revolution states that the Negro, backed by a number of whites in every section of the land, is finished with being classed as not quite human; that he is no longer humble and patient—and unlettered; and that an astonishingly large group of Negro scholars and journalists and artists are expressing their resolution with courage and skill. They are no longer "colored people." They are *people*.

Sinclair Lewis, "Black Boy (1945)," *Richard Wright: Critical Perspectives Past and Present*, Henry Louis Gates Jr., and K.A. Appiah, eds. New York: Amistad, 1993, pp. 31–32.

lence is a double-edged sword, wounding the "self" in the autobiography as it pierces a reader's consciousness of racism's systemic operations. At one level, these cultural dynamics preclude the book's being a proper target of censorship. In writing *Black Boy*, Wright intended, among other things, to exercise his First Amendment rights. He did so with such power that his book is internationally acknowledged as a classic among American autobiographies, particularly in its depiction of the forces in American society that participated in constructing, to borrow James Baldwin's marvelous phrasing, "a low ceiling of actual possibilities" for young black males. That which can be verified by the traditional, rigorous procedures of historical and sociological scholarship does not warrant censorship. It is not far afield to speculate that those who would wound Richard Wright symbolically through the censorship of *Black Boy* share some values with those who wounded the author more directly in his lifetime.

The Trussells of our world are not driven by any passionate attention to literature that may lead to the discovery of a "truth." They would have tremendous difficulty understanding that what may be profane and violent in the text of *Black Boy* is an objective correlative of the very conditions the book seeks to address. For example, Wright would not have conveyed the autobiographical truth had he written "Crush that Negro boy's testicles, Harrison!" rather than "Crush that nigger's nuts, nigger!" Instead, the Trussells of the world proceed as naive readers with God on their side, confusing parts with wholes, the surface features of a text with the thick descriptions being evoked, what is only a reference to immorality with what is genuinely so. Their motives are not literary, but they are nevertheless embroiled with interpretation and the political economy of which literature is a part. They are not seeking out proper targets for censorship (if indeed any symbolic expression can be legally censored after the 1992 Supreme Court ruling on a St. Paul, Minnesota, ordinance on hate speech and its 1989 decision regarding the Flag Protection Act), but rather any material which they deem offensive or disagreeable. Their concern is very noticeable if the material in question is used in publicly funded activities, especially in education. Those who appoint themselves guardians of public morals and social values will always provide us with occasions for justifying the potentially redemptive value of such books as *Black Boy*.

SAFEGUARDING THE FREEDOM TO REMEMBER

As we suggested earlier, much of the value of *Black Boy* is located in its providing engaging ways for us to think about how our lives are shaped by law and custom, by interracial encounters and intraracial negotiations, by desire and psychological defeat and intrepidity, by American dreams and nightmares. The entire text of *Black Boy* (*American Hunger*), now available in the Library of America edition, challenges our stereotypical thinking about South and North. In Part I, "Southern Night," the autobiographical self learns that his people "grope at noonday as in the night," believing in a better world up North. In Part II, "The Horror and the Glory," Northern exposure results in the self's "knowing that all I possessed were words and a dim knowledge that my country had shown me no examples of how to live a human life." There is no hiding place in regional differences. But what perhaps touches us most deeply, whether we are tender students or hardened adults, are the concluding words of *Black Boy:*

> I would hurl words into this darkness and wait for an echo and if an echo sounded, no matter how faintly, I would send other words to tell, to march, to fight, to create a sense of the hunger for life that gnaws in us all, to keep alive in our hearts a sense of the inexpressibly human.

In the humanistic affirmation of this conclusion is a foreshadowing of the charge several decades later to ask not what our country could do for us, but rather what we might do for our country. If *Black Boy* is read and taught intelligently as the affirmative *literary and social* critique that it is, valid reasons for wanting to censor the book will indeed be far to seek, despite the unholy alliance between the racism of the radical right and the political correctness of the conservative left. *Black Boy* is a catalyst for the freedom to remember.

Imagination Transforms Wright's Racist World in *Black Boy*

Ronald R. Primeau

Wright scholar Ronald R. Primeau of Central Michigan University writes that it is Wright's imagination, as suggested in *Black Boy*, that generates his identity and influences his vision of the world. Throughout his life, Primeau says, the tension Wright feels between "magical possibilities" and "stifling realities" produces a creative energy that helps him survive the Jim Crow laws of the South and offers hope for his future as a writer.

While *Black Boy* is essentially an account of Richard's growing realization of what it means to be black in a white world, equally important to its meaning is the unfolding of his own integrity of mind and the identity he creates for himself in order to survive and grow in a world structured to suppress his development. At two crucial points in the work Richard pauses to reflect on the contrast between the creative workings of his mind and the forces of society trying to stifle his humanity. There is a tension, for example, in his attempt to achieve his identity while learning the Jim Crow ethics: "I was in my fifteenth year; in terms of schooling I was far behind the average youth of the nation, but I did not know that. In me was shaping a yearning for a kind of consciousness, a mode of being that the way of life about me had said could not be, must not be, and upon which the penalty of death had been place." Much earlier in his experiences Richard had described more specifically the strategy he used to develop his creative sensibility and the mode of being it made

Excerpted from Ronald R. Primeau, "Imagination as Moral Bulwark and Creative Energy in Richard Wright's *Black Boy* and LeRoi Jones's *Home*," *Studies in Black Literature*, vol. 3, no. 2 (Summer 1972). Reprinted by permission of the author. (Notes in the original have been omitted in this reprint.)

possible: "My imaginings, of course, had no objective value whatever. My spontaneous fantasies lived in my mind. . . . My fantasies were a moral bulwark that enabled me to feel I was keeping my emotional integrity whole, a support that enabled my personality to limp through days lived under the threat of violence." The entire work emphasizes this role of fantasy as a creative force in Richard's growth. Interacting with and transforming his environment, Richard's imagination creates the reality that both saves him and places the penalty of death on his salvation.

THE POWER OF IMAGINATION

Richard's introspection and his creation of realities are central to the structural and thematic patterns of the work. Even in the "four-year-old days" of his life, his imagination yearns for something beyond his present reality. From the basically simple yet distinctive introspection of "my idea was growing, blooming" to his recording a series of incidents prefaced by "From that moment on things became tangled for me," Richard begins to feel the dynamics of his mind's creative energies. Very early, then, his concern with the workings of imagination leads him to nature and we find a passage reminiscent of Jean Toomer: "Each event spoke with a cryptic tongue. And the moments of living slowly revealed their coded meanings. . . . There was the delight I caught. . . . There was the faint, cool kiss of sensuality. . . . There was the yearning for identity loosed in me by the sight of a solitary ant carrying a burden on a mysterious journey." What follows this early introspection then—problems with his family and all the challenges in the neighborhood—are balanced by, and to a certain extent help produce, a sensibility in which an imaginative generation of his own identity controls his vision of the world.

Crucial structural positioning in the opening of Chapter Two underlines the central position of the growth of Richard's consciousness in the earlier years. Whereas Chapter One closes with the "city which had lifted me in its burning arms and borne me toward alien and undreamed-of shores of knowing," the beginning of Chapter Two juxtaposes the closing in and opening out of Richard's experiences: "The glad days that dawned gave me liberty for the free play of impulse and, from anxiety and restraint, I leaped to license and thoughtless action." In this frame of mind

Richard hungers for "the sharp, frightening, breath-taking, almost painful excitement" of a tale started but left unfinished by the school teacher Ella. Richard recalls how the story had been "the first experience in my life that had elicited from me a total emotional response"; it made him taste "what to me was life, and I would have more of it, somehow, someway"; it brought an increased desire for imaginative literature and the expansion of consciousness it affords: "I burned to learn to read novels and I tortured my mother into telling me the meaning of every strange word I saw, not because the word itself had any value, but because it was the gateway to a forbidding and enchanting land."

In the account that follows, Richard describes his perception of everyday realities as an immersion in experience and a rising up to challenge the unreality that he was coming to face more every day in the white world: "Each experience had a sharp meaning of its own." As "the days and hours began to speak now with a clearer tongue," Richard catalogs his sensations ("there was . . .") in a pattern of progressive discovery. The thrust of this catalog is primarily acute sensuous description. But at this time also Richard describes "the aura of limitless freedom distilled from the rolling sweep of tall green grass swaying and glinting in the wind and sun." And there are the Jim Crow lessons he must learn as when he sees the chain gang and thinks they're elephants and his mother answers his questions with "It's because . . . well, they're harder on black people."

THE SEARCH FOR MEANING

The bulk of Chapter Two, then, more than any other place in the book records the massive inconsistencies Richard confronted in his search for meaning. His questions about why so many black men wear stripes and why the black men don't fight all the white men and why the white men have guns and the black men don't are countered in his own mind by increasingly sharp sensations: "Up or down the wet or dusty streets, indoors or out, the days and nights began to spell out magic possibilities." Accordingly, the closing pages of the chapter contain an intense concentration on the workings of the mind as it transforms the impressions into new meanings: "Anything seemed possible, likely feasible, because I wanted everything to be possible. . . . Because I had no power to make things happen outside of me in the objec-

tive world, I made things happen within. Because my environment was bare and bleak, I endowed it with unlimited
potentialities, redeemed it for the sake of my own hungry
and cloudy yearning." This again is the moral bulwark of
fantasy and the intersection of the objective and the subjective at the heart of his transformation of reality. Richard's explanation of its workings gathers together all the incidents of
the first two chapters and sets up the tensions which dominate the remainder of the work. This tension between magic
possibilities and stifling realities produces fear and creative
energy in his growing use of imagination: "These fantasies
were no longer a reflection of my reaction to the white
people, they were a part of my living, of my emotional life;
they were a culture, a creed, a religion. The hostility of the
whites had become so deeply implanted in my mind and
feelings that it had lost direct connection with the daily environment in which I lived; and my reactions to his hostility
fed upon itself, grew or diminished according to the news
that reached me about the whites, according to what I as-
pired or hoped for." And Richard's Christmas that year was
as clear an indication as any of his mind's ability to savour
and stretch experience and to transform reality: "Christmas
came and I had but one orange. I was hurt and would not go
out to play with the neighborhood children who were blow-
ing horns and shooting firecrackers. I nursed my orange all
Christmas Day; at night, just before going to bed, I ate it, first
taking a bite out of the top and sucking the juice from it as I
squeezed it; finally I tore the peeling into bits and munched
them slowly."

Similarly, throughout Chapter Three Richard invests
massive meaning in the suffering his family endured, ex-
ploring its repercussions into the farthest regions of his own
consciousness and tracing its significance for his views in
later years: "My mother's suffering grew into a symbol in my
mind, gathering to itself all the poverty, the ignorance, the
helplessness; the painful, baffling, hunger-ridden days and
hours. . . . Her life set the emotional tone of my life, colored
the men and women I was to meet in the future, condition-
ing my relation to events that had not yet happened, determined my attitude to situations and circumstances I had yet
to face." And at the chapter's end he generalizes from the
concrete experiences to comment on the growth of his inner
consciousness: "At the age of twelve, before I had one full

year of formal schooling, I had a conception of life that no experience could ever erase, a predilection for what was real that no argument could ever gainsay, a sense of the world that was mine and mine alone, a notion as to what life meant that no education could ever alter, a conviction that the meaning of living came only when one was struggling to wring a meaning out of meaningless suffering." Richard's predilection for the real is a result of the interaction between his imagination and the environment his mind acts upon. And the wringing meaning out of meaningless suffering is a function of that quality of mind Ellison says critics have overlooked in the work: "They forget that human life possesses an innate dignity . . . and that all men are the victims and the beneficiaries of the goading, tormenting, commanding and informing activity of that imperious process known as the Mind—the Mind, as Valery describes it, 'armed with its inexhaustible questions.'"

Against Religion

The function of imagination in *Black Boy* helps explain from another vantage point Richard's distaste for religion. In the action of Chapters Four and Five especially, much of the unreality that moves Richard away from the reality of human experience lay in the abuses of religion. Initially he is attracted to the stimulant religion provides for his imagination: "Many of the religious symbols appealed to my sensibilities and I responded to the dramatic vision of life held by the church, feeling that to live day by day with death as one's sole thought was to be compassionately sensitive toward all life so as to view all men as slowly dying, and the trembling sense of fate that welled up, sweet and melancholy, from the hymns blended with the sense of fate that I had already caught from life. But full emotional and intellectual belief never came." Belief never comes because he discovers a basic opposition between the realities the mind sees and the distortions of consciousness perpetrated in the name of religious truth: "While listening to the vivid language of the sermons, I was pulled toward emotional belief, but as soon as I went out of the church and saw the bright sunshine and felt the throbbing life of the people in the streets I knew that none of it was true and that nothing would happen." Richard's criterion of participation in the sense of life's totality causes him to spurn his family's efforts to "save" him:

"The hymns and sermons of God came into my heart only long after my personality had been shaped and formed by unchartered conditions of life. I felt that I had in me a sense of living as deep as that which the church was trying to give me, and in the end I remained basically unaffected." Later when his mother wished to take him to God, he characterizes the methods of religion as anti-life: "This business of saving souls had no ethics: every human relationship was shamelessly exploited."

At this point, Richard's reaction against the religion of his grandmother brings him a better understanding of his own "religion" and prompts him to his first concrete manifestation of the literary impulse growing within him. He speaks now of a faith "welded to the common realities of life, anchored in the sensations of my body and in what my mind could grasp" rather than "fear of an invisible power." And he comes to realize that he has more knowledge of religion than his grandmother thinks, more about "the hunger of the human heart for that which is not and can never be, the thirst of the human spirit to conquer and transcend the implacable limitations of human life." He therefore transforms his attempts at praying into a story about Indians centering around a "yawning void": "There was no plot, no action, nothing save atmosphere and longing and death. But I had never in my life done anything like it; I had made something, no matter how bad it was; and it was mine." Contact with nature, full immersion in the things he experiences every day, conscious reflection on the workings of his mind, and his reactions against life-stifling religious attitudes come together at this time in Richard's development to produce some very early apprentice writings driven by his impulse to create and transform reality into new and more meaningful patterns.

SURVIVING JIM CROW

Structurally it is significant that Chapter Five begins with the same free impulse seen in the opening of Chapter Two—a free play smothered for those of the religious persuasion thrust upon him: "No longer set apart for being sinful, I felt that I could breathe again, live again, that I had been released from a prison. The cosmic images of dread were now gone and the external world became a reality, quivering daily before me. Instead of brooding and trying foolishly to pray, I could run and roam, mingle with boys and girls, feel at home with people, share a little of life in common with others, satisfy my hunger to be and live." And his record of the experiences that follow reveals coded meanings once more: "I was now with boys and girls who were studying, fighting, talking; it revitalized my being, whipped my senses to a high, keen pitch of receptivity."

Richard's heightened sensibility becomes at once more necessary for his survival and more difficult to develop as time goes on due to the Jim Crow Ethics that throw it into sharp contrast. In Chapters Six and Seven he describes his "mistakes" in the white world—"mistakes" that underline the wide gap between his own consciousness and what he was to be allowed in the white world: "And now a strange uncle who felt that I was impolite was going to teach me to act as I had seen the backward black boys act on the plantations, was going to teach me to grin, hang my head, and mumble apologetically when I was spoken to. My senses reeled in protest." His phrasing in the opening of Chapter Seven expresses the antipathy between his own mode of being and the Jim Crow life style. In a series of short, staccato sentences he captures the contrast between his own identity and the identity projected upon him from the white world: "Summer. Bright hot days. Hunger still vital part of my consciousness. . . . Loneliness. Reading. Job-hunting. . . . This was my reality in 1924."

But despite the Jim Crow standards, Richard's consciousness continues to expand: "The eighth grade days flowed in their hungry path and I grew more conscious of myself: I sat in classes, bored, wondering, dreaming." And he then wrote another story—published this time—but still "crudely atmospheric, emotional, intuitively psychological . . . stemmed from pure feeling." But "The Voodoo of Hell's Half-Acre" provided an outlet for his creativity; it kept his consciousness active; it once again revitalized his dreams and symbols of reality: "The north symbolized to me all that I had not felt and seen; it had no relation whatever to what actually existed. Yet, by imagining a place where everything was possible, I kept hope alive in me." In distinguishing between the dream and the reality, Richard points up once again the transforming effect of the mind in creating new realities. Even in a "country in which the aspirations of black people were limited, marked-off," he sees the fantasy-activity of his own mind doing "something to redeem my being alive."

The events that follow show Richard's need to shield his identity from the forces trying to stifle it: "The safety of my life in the South depended on how well I concealed from all whites what I felt." And it is primarily his imagination that helps him to keep his identity intact while teaching him to act out roles for survival such as the "nigger-being-a-good-boy-in-the-presence-of-a-white-man pattern." He sees into all the deliberate attempts to suppress the growth of consciousness he finds to be the meaning of life itself: "I was building up in me a dream which the entire educational system of the South had been rigged to stifle. I was feeling the very thing that the state of Mississippi had spent millions of dollars to make sure that I would never feel; I was becoming aware of the thing that the Jim Crow laws had been drafted and passed to keep out of my consciousness; I was acting on impulses that the southern senators in the nation's capital had striven to keep out of Negro life; I was beginning to dream the dreams that the state had said were wrong, that the schools had said were taboo."

INTO THE UNKNOWN

After innumerable lessons in the Jim Crow world, the story of *Black Boy* closes as Richard flings himself into the unknown, unlimited potentialities he had been nurturing throughout his early life. The most destructive element of his adjustment to the Jim Crow rules had been the degree to which "my preoccupation with curbing my impulses, my speech, my movements, my manner, my expression had increased my anxiety." But later the mode of consciousness of the early Richard returns as he describes his reading in terms of the same imaginative faculties he had earlier called the moral bulwark of fantasy: "I had once tried to write, had once reveled in feeling, had let my crude imagination roam, but the impulse to dream had been slowly beaten out of me by experience. Now it surged up again and I hungered for books, new ways of looking and seeing. It was not a matter of believing or disbelieving what I read, but of feeling something new, of being affected by something that made the look of the world different." We find, then, the mode of consciousness dominant in the earlier portions of the book becoming even more intense at the conclusion: "I held my life in my mind, in my consciousness each day, feeling at times that I would stumble and drop it, spill it forever." And his narrative closes on a note of potentialities, a need to fill up, to continue the self-conscious reflection on his own re- sponses: "I was leaving the South to fling myself into the un- known, to meet other situations that would elicit from me other responses. And if I could meet enough of a different life, then, perhaps, gradually and slowly I might learn who I was, what I might be." The ending therefore promises a con- tinuation of Richard's quest. Although there was originally more *Black Boy* at least 1/3 again as long, the ending we have (stressing possibilities in the unknown) is effective and con- sistent with the preoccupations of the work on the whole.

CHRONOLOGY

1908

Richard Wright is born on September 4 in Roxie, Mississippi. Wright's father, Nathan, is a sharecropper, and his mother, Ella, is a schoolteacher.

1910

Richard's brother, Leon, is born September 24.

1911–1912

The Wright family moves to Natchez to live with Ella's mother. Richard sets fire to his grandmother's house; he later writes about this incident in great detail in *Black Boy*.

1913–1914

After the family moves to Memphis, Richard's father abandons them. Ella works as a cook to support the family, and Richard becomes a drunkard at age six.

1916

Richard attends school for the first time, but must drop out to care for his sick mother. Richard and his brother are taken in by an orphanage for more than a month. Eventually the boys move in with maternal grandparents in Jackson, Mississippi, and then with Wright's Aunt Maggie and Uncle Silas Hoskins in Elaine, Arkansas.

1917

Richard's Uncle Hoskins is murdered by whites, another incident of focus in *Black Boy*.

1918–1919

After moving extensively, the Wrights settle again with Ella's mother in Jackson. Richard leaves his grandmother's house and moves with his brother and mother to West Helena, where she suffers a stroke. Relatives take the boys in and Ella returns to her mother's house.

1920

Richard attends the Seventh-Day Adventist school in Huntsville, Mississippi. He clashes with his Aunt Addie, the devoutly religious teacher of his class.

1921–1922

Richard enters fifth grade in Jackson and is soon advanced to sixth grade. He delivers newspapers and works with a traveling insurance salesman, two jobs he recalls with some shame in his autobiography.

1922–1923

Richard enters the seventh grade at the Smith-Robertson Public School and earns money for books, food, and clothes by running errands for whites. He develops an interest in pulp fiction and magazine stories.

1923–1924

Richard writes his first short story, "The Voodoo of Hell's Half-Acre," which is published in the black newspaper *Jackson Southern Register.*

1925

In May, Richard graduates valedictorian of his ninth-grade class. He resolves to forgo public education and to leave the deep South for Memphis.

1926

Richard works at the Merry Optical Company in Memphis in addition to his other odd jobs. He begins to read extensively.

1927–1928

Richard's mother and brother join him for a short time in Memphis; he moves on to Chicago with his Aunt Maggie. Richard works part-time for the postal service, begins to write in earnest.

1929

Begins work as a substitute clerk and mail sorter. He is writing regularly and attending meetings of black literary groups.

1930

Loses his postal job due to the stock market crash; works for a short time selling burial insurance to blacks, but is dismayed by the dishonesty of the profession.

1931

Now on state relief, Richard works for the Michael Reese Hospital and later the South Side Boys' Club and Federal Negro Theatre. Richard's second publication, the short story "Superstition," appears in *Abbott's Monthly Magazine*, a black journal. During this time, Richard gains an interest in Communist activity in the African American community.

1932

Works as an insurance salesman and a street cleaner and moves with his family into a tenement. He attends meetings of the John Reed Club, a Communist Party literary group, and begins to regularly publish poems and short stories in leftist journals.

1933

Joins the Communist Party and is elected executive secretary of the Chicago John Reed Club.

1935

Goes to New York for the American Writers' Congress, where he speaks on "The Isolation of the Negro Writer." He is hired by the Federal Writers' Project to research the history of Illinois and of the Negro in Chicago.

1936

Organizes the Communist Party–sponsored National Negro Congress and continues to write extensively. His short story "Big Boy Leaves Home" appears in the *New Caravan*, where it attracts critical attention.

1937

Turns down a permanent position with the postal service to move to New York City to pursue his writing career. He becomes the Harlem editor of the *Daily Worker* and helps launch the magazine *New Challenge*. His literary reputation begins to grow.

1938

Uncle Tom's Children: Four Novellas is published to wide acclaim. The book receives a literary prize from *Story* magazine.

1939

Receives a Guggenheim fellowship, completes *Native Son*, and marries Dhimah Rose Meadman.

1940

Native Son is published and receives national attention as a Book of the Month Club selection. Richard is estranged from wife Dhimah and has begun divorce proceedings. The success of his novel has afforded him his first taste of financial independence.

1941

Marries Ellen Poplar. *Twelve Million Black Voices: A Folk History of the Negro in the United States* is published, and *Native Son* is produced on Broadway.

1942

Daughter Julia is born.

1944

Breaks from the Communist Party and publishes a two-part article in the *Atlantic Monthly* titled, "I Tried to Be a Communist."

1945

Black Boy: A Record of Childhood and Youth is published and, like *Native Son*, is accepted by the Book of the Month Club.

1946

Visits France for the first time and feels at home in Paris.

1947

Decides to move his family to France permanently.

1949

Second daughter, Rachel, is born in January. Wright finishes a screenplay of *Native Son* and decides to play the lead character, Bigger Thomas, himself. He is unable to interest Hollywood in the script.

1950

Financial difficulties delay the filming of *Native Son* in Argentina, but the project is completed in June.

1951

Native Son opens in Buenos Aires, and thirty minutes of the film are cut by censors for the U.S. premiere on June 16. The film fails in America.

1953

The Outsider is published to mixed reviews. Wright visits the

Gold Coast (Ghana) to gather material for his book *Black Power.*

1954

Black Power: A Record of Reactions in a Land of Pathos is published along with *Savage Holiday*, Wright's only novel with all white characters. He visits Spain with interest in another writing project.

1955

Attends the Bandung Conference in Indonesia and meets with numerous world leaders to discuss Third World problems.

1956

Publishes *The Color Curtain: A Report on the Bandung Conference*, and *Pagan Spain*, based on travels in Spain. Begins a lecture tour of several European countries.

1957

White Man, Listen!, a collection of lectures, is published.

1958

The Long Dream, the first in a projected trilogy about Mississippi, is published. The book receives poor reviews and does not sell well. When Wright attempts to renew his passport, he is harassed by the American embassy for his former Communist associations.

1959

Wright's mother dies January 14. In June, Wright suffers from amoebic dysentery.

1960

A stage adaptation of *The Long Dream* opens on Broadway in February but closes in a week after poor reviews. Wright prepares more than eight hundred of his haiku for publication and begins work on a new novel. *Eight Men*, a collection of short stories, is also ready for publication. On November 28, Wright dies of a heart attack at age fifty-two; he is cremated with a copy of *Black Boy* on December 3 in Paris.

FOR FURTHER RESEARCH

BIOGRAPHY

David Bakish, *Richard Wright.* New York: Frederick Ungar, 1973.

Michel Fabre, *The Unfinished Quest of Richard Wright.* Trans. Isabel Barzun, New York: William Morrow, 1973.

Robert Felgar, *Richard Wright.* Boston: Twayne, 1980.

Addison Gayle, *Richard Wright: Ordeal of a Native Son.* New York: Anchor, 1980.

Keneth Kinnamon, *The Emergence of Richard Wright.* Urbana: University of Illinois Press, 1972.

Margaret Walker, *Richard Wright: Demonic Genius.* New York: Warner, 1988.

CRITICISM

Evelyn Gross Avery, *Rebels and Victims: The Fiction of Richard Wright and Bernard Malamud.* New York: Kennikat, 1979.

Harold Bloom, ed., *Richard Wright.* New York: Chelsea House, 1987.

Robert Felgar, *Understanding Richard Wright's* Black Boy: *A Student Casebook to Issues, Sources, and Historical Documents.* Westport, CT: Greenwood, 1998.

Yoshinobu Hakutani, *Richard Wright and Racial Discourse.* Columbia: University of Missouri Press, 1996.

Yoshinobu Hakutani, ed., *Critical Essays on Richard Wright.* Boston: G.K. Hall, 1982.

Arnold Rampersad, ed., *Richard Wright: A Collection of Critical Essays.* Englewood Cliffs, NJ: Prentice-Hall, 1995.

John M. Reilly, ed., *Richard Wright: The Critical Reception.* New York: B. Franklin, 1978.

AFRICAN AMERICAN AUTOBIOGRAPHY AND HISTORY

William L. Andrews, ed., *African American Autobiography: A Collection of Critical Essays.* Englewood Cliffs, NJ: Prentice-Hall, 1993.

Ira Berlin, ed., *Remembering Slavery: African Americans Talk About Their Personal Experiences of Slavery and Freedom.* New York: Norton, 1998.

John Hope Franklin, *From Slavery to Freedom: A History of African Americans.* New York: Knopf, 1994.

Henry Louis Gates Jr., ed., *Colored People: A Memoir.* New York: Knopf, 1994.

Leon F. Litwack, *Trouble in Mind: Black Southerners in the Age of Jim Crow.* New York: Knopf, 1998.

Crispin Sartwell, *Act Like You Know: African-American Autobiography & White Identity.* Chicago: University of Illinois Press, 1998.

Jeffrey C. Stewart, *1001 Things Everyone Should Know About African American History.* New York: Doubleday, 1997.

AFRICAN AMERICAN LITERATURE

Bernard W. Bell, *The Afro-American Novel and Its Tradition.* Amherst: University of Massachusetts Press, 1989.

Robert Butler, *Contemporary African American Fiction: The Open Journey.* Madison, NJ: Fairleigh Dickinson University Press, 1998.

Michael G. Cooke, *Afro-American Literature in the Twentieth Century: The Achievement of Intimacy.* New Haven, CT: Yale University Press, 1986.

Henry Louis Gates Jr., ed., *The Norton Anthology of African American Literature.* New York: Norton, 1997.

Carl Milton Hughes, *The Negro Novelist: A Discussion of the Writings of American Negro Novelists 1940–1950.* New York: Citadel, 1994.

Charles Richard Johnson, *Being and Race: Black Writing Since 1970.* Bloomington: Indiana University Press, 1988.

INDEX